QUARANTINE

CONFESSIONS

COMPLETE

Brody McVittie
aka
Brave Billy Ancaster
aka
really, really sorry
for the way this all turned out.

QUARANTINE

CONFESSIONS

Brody McVittie

for you,

my

mercurial

melodramatic

muse

(Mid)
MARCH.

153, 517 people infected and
5,735 killed

This COVID thing is starting
to look a little scary

like it's not just a "over
there" thing

This won't be so bad.

You move out, literally, the way
you moved out, figuratively,
some time ago.

The world goes crazy, COVID 19,
and I'm alone with my typewriter.
And my whiskey.

And my rampant, all-consuming
sadness.

What's the worst that could
happen?

APRIL.

887, 067 people infected
and 44, 264 killed

and masks in public and death-
stares at anyone who coughs

and i'm wishing you would have
at least given relative
isolation a chance

because isolating is about as
good for me as the whiskey i no
longer save for Saturdays.

leave well enough alone.

Soaked my machinations in
whiskey

and

the reservations i have for you
are relegated to the dinners
we'll never go to

again

just the name of some Kravitz
song

i sing to myself
on nights since
the night you decided
my machinations were a little
too much.

*and by the way, remember dinners out?

Fuck you, COVID.

ALL YOU LEFT ME

(WHEN YOU LEFT ME:)

-my word

-my big ol' balls

-the words i use in the stories

i tell myself

about you and the reasons you

left me.

THE SUM TOTAL OF MY DAYS, LOCKED
UP AND LOCKED AWAY IN THIS
APARTMENT:

Rumination, Proclamation, and
other Self-Important Shit.

how sad is it

```
the pics i used to get were naked
         now all i get
      are vaguely colored
         discolorations
   on zoomed-in parts of arms;

    and the scars you leave
         don't stop there
       losing big toenails
          and memories

     of times you used to
      pleasantly tease me

        instead of now
     and the just-teasings.
```

the worst part of all this:

I have to go and get my own fucking groceries.

how have you been

−OH YOU KNOW

WRITING SONGS
ABOUT YOU AND
DRINKING MYSELF TO
DEATH.

MAY.

3.2 million people infected
and 233, 000 killed

and the mask i wear
maybe keeps out the particles
that could kill me.

But the particles i'm primarily
concerned with are the particles
you left around my apartment;

the particles my mask and my
Dyson and my rampant alcoholism
can't seem to get rid of.

FIRST-TEAM ALL-DESPONDENT.

i've picked up the pen

and put down the glass

between sips and

at least long enough

to tell you the kinds of things

that maybe could have saved us

in the telling.

my name

your lips

knife turns

love hurts

sweet sounds

split lips

12 rounds

love hurts

4 letters

best words

leave now

hurts worse

you're not gonna like
this

but drugs, **am i right?**

there's abject cruelty

in the way the furniture stands still

says no/every thing, the way you used to

rocking on chairs better suited

for standing still.

IF THE GOAL IS

BOOTLEG HEMMINGWAY

HOW MANY WHISKEY NO-CHASER
SPEAR-FISHING SAFARI
BAKING SODA INFUSED EIGHT-BALLS
BEFORE A MOTHERFUCKER GETS A SHRED OF

I GET IT.

I REMEMBER
EVERY/
NOTHING
ABOUT
THE
WAY
YOU
FORGOT
ABOUT
ME.

i'm waiting in line

outside the grocery store you
used to go to for me,

and i can't help but feel
that these groceries would be
better shopped sober

and i can't help but think
that, somewhere underneath this
mask i can't really breathe in

there's a face you might maybe
miss

the way i bet you don't miss

this waiting in line shit.

mom calls

the way you won't,

and asks how i'm doing...

Resplendently lonesome.
thanks for asking.

JUNE.

6.6 million people infected
and 375,000 killed

and masks are the new beards

(as in everybody's got one)

and my usually fashion-forward
ass

is bunkered up and decidedly not
on the beaches i should be.

(and you're still gone and the
even the weather isn't making
that okay.)

all

feels

smoke

&

semi-suicidal tendencies.

you pull off

GUCCI

FENDI

those mom jeans

i never thought would come back

yeah, you're well-dressed

but nobody wears

BROKEN

quite the way i do.

STILL

like time stands

and so i can count the colors in
the eyes

i caused the tears in

and

STILL

so i can take the time it takes
to take them all back

hold you with

eyes that tell you

i love you

STILL

and

you won't need the words

because my eyes will tell you

i

always

will.

Too many years
and the times time tends to
tell the stories we tend to keep
to memories of hot tubs and
the trouble hot tubs
tend to cause.

Behaving badly
because behaving badly
is what kids where we come from
tend to:

and in all the years
and all the times
the years tend to tell
the memories i have
of the secrets I'll keep

tell me you're just like me

trouble and too

two of a kind

and of the same mind.

Going for groceries
is getting downright dangerous

and they're out of both the essentials
and the shit you used to find for the counters

and so they're dirty,
the counters,

and the lines i resort to doing
off of them

are blurring the lines in my head

trying to remember why i gave up
personal shoppers/saviors
and the self-control that maybe
came with it/you.

Saying
"i don't know anyone who is sick"

is like saying

"i don't know anyone who is sick, yet"

but the isolation that comes

with not wanting to be

is likely making me sick, staying home and playing with straws

and sipping something i swear is medicine,

but maybe better suited for teething infants and sleepless tots.

i miss mom

and i miss dad

and i miss my baby sister

and her two babies.

i miss you,

but i think we've covered that

i miss not wearing masks

and i miss the me

that didn't have to

miss any of the above.

JULY.

10, 538, 577 people infected
and 512, 689 killed

and there's this Karen at the
kiosk at the mall

and she's yelling at me

about the type of mask i'm
wearing

because we're there now

and being here now,

kiosk at the mall

is the latest battlefield
July 2, 2020 has found me
fighting/losing on.

Today's Simple
Truth

i miss you terribly.

HAVEN'T CHANGED

SINCE

SKINNED KNEES

AND

OVER-SIZED SWEAT SOCKS

(SO SIX)

AND

SO SORRY

I DON'T HAVE THE MATURITY

IT WOULD TAKE

TO NOT WRITE

EVERYTHING ABOUT YOU.

Funny how my drug dealer

is harder to get a hold of these days

but the drug dealer down the street

the one with the fucking neon

LIQUOR

sign

is about the only business open

(and business is booming.)

what should your
headstone say

HE NEVER STOPPED BEING SAD.

i've written the sentence
by the time the first word hits
the page

told the story

by the end of the first line.

i've finished the book
before the first paragraph.

i've read the first review
before i put the pen down.

i see the ending when i'm
beginning

because it is the only way

WORD ONE

ever amounts to anything

OTHER THAN.

baby, there aren't enough

Halsey songs

in the world

to tell you how disappointed i am.

what if i need you

to

NO CALLER ID

save me

AUGUST.

17 million people infected
and lots dead.

it's my birthday month and so
i'd rather not look at the
numbers.

you're calling, though, so it's a
little better than it has been,
on the whole painfully-selfish
scale i find myself (barely)
living in.

also, sun.

so that's good.

you call when it suits you

so not often

enough

for my admittedly tender/whiskey-influenced

tender little sensibilities

and

the calls are short

and your tone is too

but in lieu of progress

i'll take it like that miracle vaccine
i'm pretty sure will never come to be.

you ask, and it's

Like, Lucas Hood sad.

and you get it, because he's
that guy from that show we
liked.

(*worth a google.)

you tell me that you're doing good

and that's good

and, in passing, you tell me that normal people don't go grocery shopping every day and that i can buy enough groceries to last me, like, a week

and that's news to me

and i guess it kind of explains why Karen at Checkout Station 5 keeps looking at me funny

also, fuck Karen.

my quarterback left

and

the government won't let
me go outside

and

i'm moderately sure the
world will never be the
same...

...and

none of this ruined me

the way you did

-inspiring the next/rest

every word and every

lack of

rest

with just one simple
call.

ABSCONDED WITH YOUR ATTENTIONS.

it's my birthday (!)

and it's a little different this year and i don't feel like celebrating

and there's a sick world outside my window

and you're on the phone, which is something

but i'm blowing out candles metaphorically this year,

all isolated in august and wishing

the work i'm putting into the words

was working a little faster.

I REMEMBER WHEN

REMEMBER

wasn't a four
letter word.

w h y ?

...because phantom pain

is the best pain.

SEPTEMBER.

26, 121, 999 people infected
and 864, 618 killed

and i'm shopping for the kinds
of things i hope will win you
back and

i think Karen is staring at me
but i can't tell,

her new mask is hidden by the
fogged-up face-shield she's
fogging up

and the kids are back to
school and decidedly not back
to school shopping

this year staying weird, all
empty malls and tactical-
looking kiosk operators.

FUNNY HOW I WAS EVERY

GOOD

FOUR LETTER WORD

AND THEN I WAS EVERY

BAD

FOUR LETTER WORD

AND NOW I'M ON MY BACK;

LIKE

LOVE

ME

FUCK

ME

... **CALL**

ME.

I THROW WORDS AT YOU

the biggest words i know
the smallest words with the
hidden meanings

words to boast about the man i am
words to hide the man i'm not

words that fall
deaf ears
unnecessarily parted lips

because the second i see you
the words i've said

mean nothing to the words
unsaid.

well, you know i'm always around
and willing to take it farther
than we maybe should.

WHY IS WAITING OUTSIDE AND IN LINE
AT THE LIQUOR STORE

NOWHERE NEAR THE PAINFUL
OF WAITING OUTSIDE AND IN LINE
AT THE GROCERY STORE?

3 Parts Hurt

2 Parts Whiskey

1 Part Disdain for the basic nature of Self-Preservation

...the perfect recipe for
 the kind of doom girls
 like you kinda go for.

YOU SAID
SEVENTEEN SOMETHINGS

TEN
SOUNDED KINDA SWEET

SIX
I REMEMBER EVERY SOUND OF

ONE
MADE ME FORGET FOR A MOMENT

THAT EVERY MOMENT WITHOUT

THE SOUND OF THAT SEVENTEENTH SOMETHING

WOULD RING IN MY EARS

LONG AFTER

PROVERBIAL RINGS LEFT SUPPOSED FINGERS.

I'M SOMEHOW BOTH

STAY AWAY

and

STILL

SYNONYMS IN THE HYMNS
YOU ONLY SING
TO YOURSELF.

i stay on pages

and

i never let go of anything

so

you're good, as far as

unrequited longings go.

so i'm equal parts

get you back
don't die

the way i have been
since corona was
just the beer i
passed in favor of
something stronger.

OCTOBER.

34, 495, 176 people infected
and 1, 025, 729 killed

and this is getting the kind
of old

that birthday back in August
tells me i am too.

YOU'RE THE KIND
WHO'S REALLY JUST NOT;

BLESSED WITH A BODY BETTER THAN

SOMEHOW LESS IN YOUR MIND

AND THE COST TO ME

AND MY INSATIABLE THIRST FOR THE
PICS THAT PROVE IT

IS DAYS WITHOUT MESSAGES
AND THEN MESSAGES WITHOUT NUDES

AND YOU IN THEM.

here's a little poem
i wrote you

corona is better when it's
beer

and

life was better when you were
here.

SPOOKY

LIKE HOW I'M ON YOUR MIND TONIGHT .

HAPPY HALLOWEEN

SINCERELY

-YOUR FAVOURITE GHOST,
THE ONE THAT HAUNTS YOU

(AND NOT JUST ON HOLIDAYS.)

GROWING UP I THOUGHT
GEORGE MICHAEL

WAS AS STRAIGHT AS A STRAIGHT MAN
GREW UP TO BE

AND

I MIGHT HAVE BEEN OFF ON THAT ONE

BUT

I'M ONE WHISKEY AWAY

FROM COMING OUT OF QUARANTINE

WITH A DANGLING CROSS EARRING

AND A PENCHANT FOR CHASING EVERYTHING
WITH DADDY ISSUES

LIKE IT'S 1987

cooped up
since
cooped up
was
coffee
and

cooked up
schemes
on how to get
cooped up
with
you.

locked up

and

the hurt is from

stubbed toes

empty fridges

you

the ghost in the graveyard
these four walls became
some days south of quarantine
still north of comfortable.

HAUNT ME

i'm proud of
the spiral i threw senior year

the car i stole to get to that party
(-*allegedly*)

the twist of tongue i could
form the words to fool you.

or girls like you
on some catchy pop song shit

because you
(and those cops back when)

never quite fell
for the sincerity i mixed

in and around the words to hide
the ways you terrified me.

SO THE LEAVES ARE TURNING
AND THE DAYS ARE GETTING SHORTER

AND THE LINES ARE GETTING LONGER

AND THE NEWS SAYS FLU SEASON MEANS
COVID SEASON, TIMES TWO

AND THE TIMING IS ALL WRONG, BECAUSE
I COULD USE MORE

TIME

TO WRITE THE REST OF THIS AND
BECOME THE KIND OF GUY THAT CAN
DRINK LESS AND SELL MORE AND

BECOME THE KIND OF FAMOUS
THAT I STILL THINK I DESERVE TO BE.

NOVEMBER.

46 million people infected
and 1.2 million killed

and there are rumblings of
lockdowns and restricted
movements and there's a good
chance everywhere but the
grocery store i begrudgingly
go to will be closed

again

and before the snow falls, i've
got to write the poem or say
the words that will get you
back.

because i'm tired of going for
groceries.

you said my name in my sleep

and my eyes opened.

i'm scared of
heights
rattlesnakes
covid-anything

i worry about losing
my mom
my hair
my semblance of the fragile ego i
cling to

since clinging to you
became something i just do
metaphorically now:

something i really want to
even though i'm really

most scared
of you.

Here's something better kept to myself:

you scheme with the subtelty of a sound-cloud rapper

but when it comes to lies told with twisted tongues

you're fucking with Annie Lennox.

·educate yourself hoe.

There's no predictable pattern
to your errant unpredictability

and me and my
tender sensibilities
would prefer you not catching
my more embarrassing moments

in and around
the (only) moments
your errant unpredictability
chooses to
remember i made you that way.

BURNING BRIDGES WORSE THAN
DINNER

AND I CAN BLAME

THE BARBECUE
THE CHICKEN

YOU

ANYTHING OTHER THAN
THE TRUTH OF THE MATTER:

I COOK ABOUT AS WELL
AS I
CO-HABITATE.

i pay
compliments and for purses
paying for that one thing
i never really can:

prices north of
that last thing with all them zeroes
attached

all them

except the one i took
and on the chin

letting you close that door behind you.

Threw me under the bus
like i lined up against Bettis:

36 ways they did me
the kind of dirty that doesn't
come out of sheets

and between them
was where we lived before

rumors and rantings and
screenshots

blew me up harder
than
the drywall you put my coffee cup
through.

you remember
a laundry list of faults

respectable, mountain-sized
flaws

you fail to forget

i loved you

more than sweaters fresh out the
dryer.

you mind
a lot less than you think you do

and yours is filled
with the kind of dark

you swear my writing is too:

so we're the same
connected by the kind
that really kinda isn't

one reason
amongst the other 138
we can't stay away

the way you swear we need to.

DECEMBER.

61.8 million people infected
and 1.4 million killed

Boxing Day mandatory
lockdowns

so Christmas isn't what it
used to/should be

and there's nothing under the
tree i don't have

and the chances of you
jumping out of a big, brightly
wrapped box are fading faster
than my sobriety.

♥ I STILL ♥

like all your photos
and
i still
sing all your songs

and
not the way we used to
but

the tune i can't carry

weighs
way less than the baggage that weighs
and waits

by the door
you left yours by.

it's crazy

you can say
something

so simply:

send the sparks

behind the knees and
to chests

charge
that thing i try to
keep

locked up behind
(rib) cages.

TURNED YOUR WORDS INTO
W_INE...

AND

ALL I HAD TO DO WAS GET THE (H) OUT.

you swear you don't remember

and i swear i don't remember

but sunset car rides

have burned a place

in the memories that remind me

forgetting you was

something i swear i'll never do.

you're at least every-other thought,
and all of the restless ones

every late-night indulgence
and the sum total of my lost words
and misguided attempts at
explanation

you're things unsaid
and the soft parts i keep buried

but buried is only
until your eyes meet mine

and then you own them,
and the spaces between
leaving "other"

just another failed attempt
to think any thought unattached to
you.

Merry Christmas!

and it's really anything but this year
because we're locked down starting tomorrow,
and you're nowhere near willing to come back to the place you ran from

so the presents under the tree
are just for me

and there's no need to wrap them
because they're really not there
anyways.

weekends go by
and you're anywhere else
and tonight's a Saturday
and that same bar is holding
you down

the way i used to.

so while you're collecting
attention
i'm catching the kinds of feels
it takes to write this,

one more page
until i'm done and famous

and everywhere else
but that same bar
that'll still be holding you
down.

764, 260 vaccines administered worldwide

some are excited, some are skeptical; if being stabbed in the arm means i can eventually roam outside the constraints of my four walls

i'll take the two i apparently need to

and be back to making horrible decisions regarding you

or girls just like you.

i came into this world ugly
and so i handle things the same

and meningitis couldn't kill me
the way that girl tried way
back when

so it's ugly but it works,
somehow
and i'm still here

although i apologize for the
way this starts

i can try my damndest to see it
doesn't end that way

if you'll wait me out
the way catastrophic childhood
diseases
and homicidal exes couldn't

i'm sorry

christmas has me all fucked up this year.

JANUARY.

80, 326, 479 people infected
and 1, 831, 703 killed

so Happy New Year!

(but not really)

because we were all hoping
the '1' on the end of 202_

would turn the page on this
shit,

and we'd be miraculously
cured and far better off

instead of the not better off

we so very clearly are.

climbing walls like cliffs
because imagination is outdoors, now

gone

the way of
favorite QB's on favorite teams

large gatherings

you

leaving me

to memories of outdoor spaces

championship runs

and

any hope of tomorrow being half the fun
of the ones before

walls were cliffs

and

outdoors was something more than

something people speak fondly in
remembrance of.

so your socials tell me
you're maybe seeing somebody new

/else

and as you can tell by the pages that
preceded this,

i'm clearly equipped to deal with it.

but hey,

New Year-New You

right?

i hate

settle

the way you hate

football

off-brand shoes

me

and i'm not mad you did

settle

so you have receding hairline him

and i'll keep

writing the words

that cause the storms

that still kill you.

words like

indifferent

will never be among the words
you feel when you feel things
about me

too many letters and too much
thinking of how to spell them

too much, taking away from the
thinking and of four-letter
words you'd rather

the way you'd rather just think
about me.

You're worth
the head trauma
and subsequent scars

the sleepless nights
and the ones i wish were,

dreaming it turned out different
and
waking up to

the marks i made
to remind me.

MORE BAGGAGE THAN TERMINAL 3.

♥ HEY ♥

i realize this reads fast

and i suppose last year went by the same,

locked up and longing

this year realizing you've maybe moved on

the way you moved out

some 117 pages ago.

*And i really should get over this,

but you're lingering like the pandemic

and i can't fully blame it

for keeping me from the outside world.

FEBRUARY.

102, 399, 513 people infected
and 2, 217, 015 killed

so Happy Valentine's Day!

(but not really)

because we're still locked
down and locked up

and it's way less fun in
winter,

and winter kinda feels like
it's never gonna end

the way COVID kinda feels the
same.

THIS MONTH FEELS A LITTLE ROUGHER THAN USUAL

AND THAT'S SAYING SOMETHING,
AND I AM

AND I FIGURE IT'LL BE SPRING 2045

BEFORE I'M OVER THIS

THE WAY I'M OVER THIS.

Five million vaccines
administered worldwide

and whether you believe in them or
not, we're nowhere near getting one

because the shortages are
everywhere and the doses needed
are two

and one seems like it'll be forever

and the three, particularly
concerning variants have me
thinking

that as soon as there is hope on the
horizon

COVID kicks me right in the balls.

HELP, PLEASE

whiskey and worst behavior
hand in hand

metaphorically and maybe not
literally

but the vibe i'm putting out
there
because i can't be out there

is the kind of toxic
my liver most assuredly is.

Happy Valentine's Day!

and you ARE with someone new

and it's the not-okay it has been

but, in light of global events

and pandemics comma plural

i'll take it on the chin

and wash it down with something strong

and thank you for the best-seller you'll inevitably help me write .

ALL OF THIS IS EXHAUSTING.

tired of being

tired

maybe less rampant alcoholism

maybe more first-team all hopeful

because the former

resulted in a year wasted

and the latter

is all that's left.

the sun hits the snow

and everything kind of glows:

and it's minus one hundred something

but in lieu of darker days

i'll take the cold

over the closed-in

of closed-in rooms

and the thoughts that follow.

i'm at the grocery store
and

there's this girl in line
and

she doesn't smile like you

but she smiles, behind her mask
and

for the first time in forever

maybe

in line at the grocery store

isn't the worst thing in the world.

Lockdown is over (!)

for now, and i'll take it

Spring coming

Summer coming
(and over for dinner!)

Summer because that's her name

the girl from the line at the
grocery store

the first of the maybe-good-
for-me things i'll take to get
over you.

(Mid)
MARCH.

lots of people infected and
too many killed

and for the first time in a
year, i'm not obsessing over
numbers

focused and on summer

summer in winter

the way it's been summer

since the fall

i fell for you.

you moved out, literally, the
way you moved out,
figuratively, a long time ago.

The world is still crazy,
COVID 19, but i'm not alone
with my typewriter anymore.

And my whiskey is rare now
and shared on occassion.

My sadness stays, sometimes,
and that's okay--because it's
no longer rampant and all-
consuming and always
directed at you.

The worst has happened,
and i'm still here.

BONUS

SOME MARCH IN THE FAR FUTURE

27.5 zillion infected and way way too many killed

and you're married and you have like 2.5 kids or something

and you're happy and i'm

relatively

happy

relatively, because Bon Jovi told me a long time ago that a poet needs the pain

and COVID 239 keeps me somber and motivated

the way you and the whiskey i
now stay away from

whisper to me from across
time and the places

time keeps whispering in my
good ear.

time heals all wounds.
*REMIXES

she said she thought about me

on her wedding day

and i don't have the clever

to turn the phrase

the way that particular knife does;

side

not worth showing

but rest assured

there's been little

just the thought that follows

the last thing she said

before words were ghosts

and days without weddings.

look, i'm not saying
those kids don't love you with
all their hearts...

...i'm just saying they don't love
you more.

i can only think of two things
you maybe love more than me

(and i bet it's still close)

because when you close your eyes
i can't think of one you see
in your mind and the dreams
you don't mind dreaming

the ones you have all the time
and still not even close

to how often i dream of you, too.

still   🔍

~~END.~~

*NEVER

Ketamine

QUARANTINE

CONFESSIONS

2
x

the fun of
(sober) volume
1

Broddy McUttic

WARNING
(−in lieu of a preface)

Never really one
for semblance of structure
or perfect plot

and so
apologies;

while Quarantine Confessions 1
(--on sale now)

had a narrative more
representative of what you might
commonly find

in books like these

--this one,
Quarantine Confessions 2
follows the completely non-
sensical

non-direction

of this fucking Pandemic

no end in sight

and more exhausting than
it has any right to be.

PART ONE

Poems for Being Sad.
(In a Global Pandemic.)

JUNE.
(The second June since this
whole mess started.)

171 million infected and
3.7 million killed

and I swore I wouldn't obsess
about numbers anymore

but I also swore I wouldn't
obsess about you

and we both know my ability
to be honest

pales in comparison to my
ability to both write and
obsess,

and so here I am

doing my part to ensure
you're filled with stats and
longings.

FUCK PAGE NUMBERS,
THIS IS ONE OF THOSE
CONVENTION BE DAMNED
PUT-THE-TENDER-SENSIBILITIES-TO-BED
PAGE TURNERS

SO
DOG EAR THE ONES ABOUT YOU AND
WONDER WHAT I WAS THINKING

THE FIRST TIME I READ IT BACK AND TOO

AND THEN WONDER WHAT YOU'LL BE THINKING
THE FIRST TIME I READ IT TO YOU.

*some of this is about you
some of this is about her
and
--as much as it kills you
one or two are about *her*

i'll leave it up to you
and the rest of the readership
to decipher semi-well-intentioned
meanings
behind words, mean and otherwise
that mean more to some
than o**ther**s.

Okay, so I haven't written
since the last booked wrapped,

(mid)
MARCH

and the madness supposed/not
really ended lockdowns wrought.

So here we are, and it's later
and the lockdown is gonna end
(FOR REAL THIS TIME!)

and I'm walking to the clinic
and for my very first poke,

and all I can think of

is you and

the mess losing you cost me and
the rest of the world.

So it's June
300 million doses, here

and it may be one, and it may be two
and admittedly I'm not great at
reading data

like I'm not great at reading signs
like the signs I should have read

the signs that read

DANGER

well before some fucking virus
stopped my world

the way you were dying to.

I've had it
with girls named after seasons

they last almost as long
as their collective namesakes;

and so, for Christ's sake
could I meet someone
with half the staying power

of fucking seven-seasons
You.

LOOK, I NEVER REALLY UNDERSTOOD THE PHASES
BUT I'M TOLD TWO NEEDLES AND A COUPLE TENDAYS

AND WE'RE OUT OF THIS MESS
THE WAY WE REALLY NEED TO BE

BECAUSE

OUR FAVORITE RESTAURANT CLOSED
AND I'LL NEVER SEE MY BARBER AGAIN

AND THE WORLD WE'RE INHERITING
DOESN'T LOOK LIKE THE WORLD WE PUT ON PAUSE

AND SO PAUSES
CAN JOIN PHASES

ON MY LIST OF THE EVER-INCREASING
WORDS WE ARE NOT ALLOWED TO SAY.

TAMMY

according to her name tag,

is my injection specialist.

And it's not fun,
like Botox
or Heroin

but she's all I've got
and so it's Moderna
or Pfizer

and naps

so I can get back to
the comforts of
Heroin
and poems about you.

The needle goes in and

I suppose I'm supposed to feel something

but

I'm as numb to the vaccine
coursing through my veins

as I am ambivalent to the
situation I find myself in

alone in self-imposed
apocalypse

and no one
to commiserate over
ice-cream and brain-frozen
semi-serious schemes.

The news tells me

I'm likely to grow a third eye

and I'm all for it,

perspective and wisdom and

the things third eyes bring

less concerned about side-effects than the ability to weaponize freedom

and go places other than the liquor stores

your absence

and this apocalypse

have left me infrequently frequenting.

My status

--according to my status card

tells me I'm eligible for the second poke

significantly faster than the non-status

status of the person beside me.

And I'll take it

despite the whispers that

individuals sharing my status get fast-tracked for reasons

rhyming with schmexperimental

because the hopeless romantic in me

appreciates the government-issued

free heroin/whiskey/ketamine of it all.

She tells me I might be a little sore,

Tammy does

And I just look at her and laugh

A poke and pandemic syrup

has nothing on

the needles I use

to cope with isolation

and

you.

2.9 billion vaccines
administered worldwide

and I'm one of them, now

thanks to Tammy and her

'you call that a needle'

needle

and I'm on the fast track for dose two

and on the way home to make horrible decisions

decidedly related to you.

SCARY HOURS ARE THE ONLY HOURS I KEEP.

in case I don't feel good

following the steps I take

in confidence and the semi-
promised assurances

we can have our world back;

on some of these pages

to remind you,

in case the poem on this page

is the last semi-good-faith scribble

my scrambled mind can scribble.

(mid)
JUNE.
(And the delerious rants of a
post first poked mind)

Call me Mr. Moderna

better in doses

decidedly smaller

so read these

a page or two at a time

any more

and I'll have you

laid out

feverish

and reading a little more into it

than you most assuredly should.

THE FEVER HITS

AND IT'S LESS VACCINE

AND MORE THE KETAMINE/WHISKEY I CHASE IT WITH;

AND MY FREQUENT LAPSES
IN BOTH JUDGMENT AND MENTAL HEALTH

HAVE ME ERASING THE PROGRESS
I MAKE IN QUARANTINE CONFESSIONS VOLUME ONE

LESS FUN

THAN THE MAL-INTENTIONED MACHINATIONS OF THIS

THE FIRST SEQUEL BETTER THAN THE ONE BEFORE.

you ask how long I'll love you

and it's forever

and at least all of the everydays within it

as long as we have

you'll remember the love

long after questions fade

and time takes

all of the everything-else it can have

love that's left

all that's left

and more than enough.

Fuck you,

I'll take

Old Soul

over

No Soul

any day of the week.

TOXIC YEAH

BUT IN A FUN WAY.

i care a lot less

about the money I'll never make

the cars I'll never drive

the places I'll never go;

I care a lot more

about the things i would have bought you

the backseat of the car i would have given them to you in

Uber'd up around some island i only visit

in dreams i only always dream about you

I'd trade all six of my abs

and all forty of my (fucking forty already)

years

for two and a half more with you.

Like maybe we could make up for

the two and a half we maybe kinda wasted,

all rampaging insecurities

and the kind of mind-blowing makeup sex

rampaging insecurities make worthwhile.

You're bad with scissors
and carefully crafted words.

You're worst on Wednesdays --
i guess getting over that particular hump
was always made harder by my fucking
selfish ability to just kind of be around.
So put down the pointy things
take the breath you were saving
for the yelling you're about to--
because that Wednesday night show is about
to start
and punching holes is better saved for the
plotlines.

STOP ME

IF YOU'VE HEARD THIS ONE

I'M NOT OVER IT.

write,

hope it resonates,

wait.

you know

and I know

this shit will hit different when I'm dead

so waiting

is about as effective

as telling you to read this

and the rest

I've lost rest

hoping you'll care enough to read.

ALL SOLD OUT OF SELF PRESERVATION
AND THE SORT OF THING

THAT SHOULD PROBABLY PREVENT

THE NEXT PAGE

AND THE PAGES THAT FOLLOW.

Fuck you,

Have this one for free,

it's not like you'd pay for it

(the way you're gonna pay for it on every single one of these pages)

anyways.

And anyways,

enjoy ;)

Keep all your

Red-State Desert Heat Baby-Factory

Indignations

Aimed squarely at

the Anybody-else you could almost get to

take you and those criminally blue eyes

back.

You're lucky I chose

POEMS NO ONE READS

over the (now, in hindsight

infinitely more profitable)

SONGS EVERYONE BOPS.

No machine to push this

None of the trendier ethnicities

or de jeur gender pronouns

just good old fashioned, cancel-worthy rage

and disdain for the kind of heart that could break

such an easily breakable heart.

Low-key Savage

since 21

and 21

(minus 1)

older now

means that while I still

love a good Bieber song,

I'm burdened by both

the beasts and beats

Mick and maybe Jon Bon wrote about

These Days

spent reminiscing about

those days.

JULY.
(And just in time for Jab Two.)

182 million infected and
3.9 million killed

and maybe I'm numb to the numbers

but that first jab didn't kill me

the way you and COVID seem to want to,

and the alone you've both left me to be

is about to close

the way we're about to (hopefully)

open.

Almost a year off,

One corporate call in

And I'm ready for the world to

Shut the fuck down again.

REGRET IS A FUNNY THING.

LIKE RELIGION.

The older I get the more I realize

biology betrays

chemistry stays

like I should have loved science

A little maybe more than I did

A little less time admiring

A little more time investigating

Why I found you so irresistible too

Chalking it up

the way foolish boys do

to the dark of your hair

over the particles inside

the eyes I appreciated

at least as much as mine.

DON'T GO TO BED BROKEN

—FIRST/LATEST IN A LINE OF RULES I'M INTENT ON BREAKING TONIGHT AND EVERY OTHER.

I always required

a degree of patience

a modicum of pity

at least a rudimentary understanding of circumstance

circumstance, my favorite four-letter word

when it comes to

the humility you so bravely displayed

in the painfully short years worth of encounters

that made it painfully obvious

dealing with me was a little more than

advertised on my cleaner surfaces.

So, to recap

CHEMISTRY > BIOLOGY

Math Science class couldn't teach me half as good as you did.

I'm back at work and it's working

wonders for an admittedly
shattered state of mind,

and I don't

mind

being around people,

even if being around people

means being around their wildly
inaccurate opines on the reasons
why

they're either jabbed or not jabbed

and while logic
and the need to get back to some
state of norm

dictates being back under the
oppression of corporate life

is necessary too,

I can't help but wonder

If wildly inaccurate opines
are as part of the 'new normal'

as faces hidden

the way intentions used to be.

I failed famous
like Grade 10 math
and there's a chance

IF YOURE READING THIS

I failed you, too
and so

*IF YOURE READING THIS ITS
TOO LATE*

like I should have dropped a
mixtape,

and you should have skipped
this story.

RUMINATIONS

MACHINATIONS

&

other big words

from a tiny mind.

To be fair,
I was writing about
my mental health

unhealth

about twenty before it was trendy

so I turn a phrase
like you turn a back

and I twist tongues, cool
you curl yours

and toes
in the sheets you twist and turn

twisting up schemes
to fix your mental

unhealthy

ability
to waste time missing

--more than my writing.

13 books

20 years

627 chapters

1345 poems

1, 307, 642 words

0 flowers.

(so give me those.)

*while I'm still living.
**pretty please.

still

&

stay

&

all of the words my eyes tell you.

DRIVE AWAY

PRETEND IT DOESN'T KILL YOU A
LITTLE BIT, TOO.

Days and days go by
and
the absence of you
lingers
in a way I wish your ghost would.

Hauntings metaphorical
and
not half the fun

of peering down half-lit halls
and
wondering what corner
you're handsomely hiding behind.

The hair you left
on hardwood floors

(*the hair I swore I'd never finish
cleaning up)

is conspicuously absent too

And so the days that pass
are cleaner;

but half the fun
of the hiding you and that damn
hair

used to haunt me

down hallways and the cracks
between floorboards.

Softer than

the cookies you used to bake

on Friday nights

better suited for baking.

The half-baked

writing I'm doing now

about as half-hearted

as the effort you put back into me

forever envious

of those goddamned cookies.

I've run out of

-creative expression
-good taste
-patience

And so maybe this

is the totality

of the little that's left;

Half-hearted musings

of the half you took

leaving me to the ramblings

I scribble on the pages

you maybe only care to read

Running, and in

decidedly opposite directions.

OKAY, YOU'RE RIGHT

KNOWING YOU'RE SOMEWHERE FUMING ABOUT IT

WAS AT LEAST HALF THE REASON I WROTE

THAT LAST LITTLE THING I WROTE ABOUT YOU.

I turn to the whiskey
Because the world is still shut off

And although I've done my part
I'm told to wait until the malcontents do theirs

And so

I turn to the whiskey
And it whispers to me
And in the talking

The "where have you beens"
Become "hey, remember her?" 's

And I'm back on the sauce
And I'm thinking

Maybe I'm The Sauce, too

And so I'm calling you
The way the liquid courage
And the rampant loneliness

Have me calling you

...And the rest of this book that follows

Follows my inability to deal with

The pick up or don't

You're most certainly about to.

Mr. Misgiving.

If there's 1 thing Rambo 2 taught me,

it's that burying my sadness

under peptide-accelerated tans and an aggressively ridiculous lack of body fat

is the best way to deal with

the PTSD of losing

You and the latest

of the losing things

me and my moderately unhealthy tan

are resigned to.

Really, it's your fault

For loving badly broken boys.

I went to the fridge
to grab
the last of the cookies you baked

I made the mistake of bringing my
notebook with me

five poems & one still open door later

I'm ten crumbs & half a lightbulb away
from

the exasperating existentialism that
comes

when the last of the cookies go

the way of fridge lightbulbs
and the pride it takes
to put down the pen
and pick up the phone
and thank you
at the very least
for the savory sweetness that lingers
knowing I'll never eat cookies again.

If you're looking for

emotionally stunted,
scared little boys

who puff their chests out trying
to be anything else,

You've come to the right place.

YOU GO IN THAT SPECIAL PLACE
LIKE MY DOG DABBER FROM WHEN I
WAS SIX

A PERFECT MEMORY

AND THE KIND OF PRESENT

THAT MAKES EVERY PULLING OF
THAT FIRST LEG

THROUGH THE PANTS I'M HOPING
WILL CARRY ME THROUGH THE DAY

JUST A LITTLE MORE PAINFUL

THAN STARTING ANOTHER DAY
HAS ANY RIGHT TO BE.

2 many million infected and
2 many million killed

and it's white noise to me
now
because it kinds feels like
I'm getting my world back
and while getting my world
back should maybe mean you

I'll that the reemergence of
the economy and a modicum of
normality in the interim

to be spent scheming schemes
on how to make their lack of
restrictions (relatively
speaking)

last longer than we had any
right to.

GET OVER IT

ALL OVER AGAIN.

I'm early, in terms of time wasted

waiting for that second poke,

Vaccine injection #2 coming faster

than half-believed promises

of days with indoor activities in them,

seeing people for the first time

in what has been a long time,

and the one person I can' t wait to see

is the one person who maybe meant it

when they said they never really want to

see me

DELORES

according to her name tag,

is my injection specialist.

And it's not fun,
like Sodomy
or Heroin

but she's all I've got
and so it's Moderna,
again

and more naps

so I can get back to
the comforts of
Heroin
and poems about you.

The needle goes in and

I suppose I'm supposed to feel something this time

and

maybe I'm a little less numb to the vaccine
coursing through my veins

a little less alone in self-imposed
apocalypse

knowing maybe no one
to commiserate over
ice-cream and brain-frozen
semi-serious schemes

is as temporary
as the supposed pain from this
supposed last needle.

I've got friends

(--believe it or not)

that are violently anti-vax

and while part of me wants to support
the likely misbegotten concept of personal freedom

the part of me that wants
you and the ability to see you

across tables and in decidedly public places

quietly hopes

they'll join me and the rest of the so-called 'sheep'

in doing our part to keep 2020
in the past where it fucking should be.

STUFF CAN OPEN

IT SAYS ON THE NEWS

AND SO I'M HOPING

IN THE OPENING

YOU TAKE MY AGGRESSIVELY OPEN

INVITATION

TO INVITE YOURSELF

INTO MY SWEAR-IT'S-DIFFERENT-THIS-TIME

WORLD

THE ONE I HOPE
A CONVENIENTLY TIMED GLOBAL CRISIS

LEFT YOU ROSE-COLORED IN THE
REMEMBERING.

PART TWO.

Poems for Becoming Infatuated.
(In a Global Pandemic.)

August.
(and not just everything after.)

198 million infected and
4.2 million killed

and summer has me pretending
any of that is okay,

because I'm allowed to go
places for the first time in
tiny forevers

but why would I want to,
isolation and outright
apathy fighting summer sun
outside,

outside allegedly 'okay'
again.

Passports
to go anywhere

but

there's nowhere to go

now
where

would I be
without isolations
self-imposed or otherwise;

and so the restaurants & bars
can stay open

the bars I stay behind
caged in a mind I made up

long before passports
and external circumstances.

People are losing
jobs & sanity
and you can feel it on the
streets

fender bendings & raised
voices

reserved for forums
where both reservations &
decorum

demand anything but

but the faith I have
in the humanity I lost
tells me we'll be okay

and I'm not,
but hey

--they can't all be about me
the way they're all about
you.

Manifested

Misery

&

Malintent

'Someday'

is a trigger.

I ALMOST GAVE UP
ON SOME
'WHY NOT GIVE UP'
SHIT;

THE WHISKEY WHISPERED
REMINDERS THAT

OF ALL THE THINGS
I'M REALLY JUST NOT
I'M REALLY JUST NOT
THE ONE TO QUIT

THE WAY YOU AND MY SOBRIETY
COULDN'T WAIT TO.

I take my coffee

the way you took

my rational ability

to just kind of get by

and I am,
you know,

getting by
and barely

wanting to less

because you left me
to stronger coffee

and the kind I have to
make my own damn self.

It's Orwellian,
this dystopia we find ourselves
in,

or it's not
1984

nothing to you
save one admittedly really good
Taylor Swift album

some thirteen years
before you came around

and some thirteen months
since this dystopia

(maybe)
weighed on you enough

to make you
and your pop-informed decisions

worthy of memory holes

and

the kind you punched clear
through me

totalitarian

in your ability

to take a globally bad situation

and

somehow make it worse.

I'm sick of writing
about pandemics and the pain that
comes with it

as you are,
reading too many pages like this one

desperately lonesome

and desperately writing
in the hopes

that hope
is enough

to do something about
the latest of things

I'm sick of having no control over.

Regret?

Volumes worth,

the latest & last

you hold in the hands

I'd much rather

hold me.

Unquestionably Underrated

&

Appropriately Unconscionable.

I SWORE I WAS DONE

QUARANTINE CONFESSIONS 1

BUT YOU LEFT

ME TO FOURTH WAVES

AND WAVING GOODBYE

OUT WINDOWS

OTHERSIDE OF THE WALLS

THE GOVERNMENT PREFERS I HIDE BEHIND.

SO

QUARANTINE CONFESSIONS 2

AND

FUCK YOU.

Vaxx

or

No Vaxx

you're all assholes

to me.

The ring I didn't
wasn't the ring I wouldn't
you just assumed
the way I did,
believing you
when you told me
you didn't/wouldn't.

So lie
the way you did,
wonder why I shouldn't.

I almost gave up
on some
"why not give up"
shit;

the whiskey whispered
reminders that

of all the things
I'm really just not

I'm really just not

the one to quit

the way you and my sobriety
couldn't wait to.

Your eyes
don't make sense
&
your ass
is the one-of-a-kind

those prescription-weak glasses

only reflect

the subtleties my gaze
clearly lacks

looking back at you
&
those eyes
&
that ass
&

wondering why I ever bothered to
write about anything else.

I'm back at the liquor store
and it's weird because we're
allowed to go places now,

and while I'm actually kind of
happy to see

somewhat normal people join me in
the quest to medicate themselves,

I can't help but feel

things being open

is as now-strange

as this being decidedly-not

used to be.

You're looking at me,

all eyes-that-don't-make-sense

and I can't

make sense of the reasons you're choosing to fix a gaze better suited

(literally) any-elsewhere

at me and my not-even-broken-toy cute

suffering personage.

I'll take it,

as Hail Mary salvations go,

you and those eyes

&

that ass

suited to saving

decidedly more

than the last sip of whiskey

we're suddnenly sharing

atop couches previously suited

for isolations and abject sadness.

September.

218 million infected and
4.5 million killed and

...fuck this.

Fuck it

I'm taking a month off
because things are open and
maybe not for long

but this month
writing about feelings means
feeling them

and the sunshine in the world-
there-still-is outside

means I'd rather be out there

and I'd rather just not.

I took September off

and so sorry that chapter sucked

I promise to make it up to you

the way all the words

in all the books

kinda just couldn't.

Gobtobler.

234 million infected and
4.8 million killed

and it's still kinda summer
outside and summer has a way
of fooling us into thinking
it's okay

and it's really still kinda
anything but

okay

and here's really fucking
hoping this coming fall

is the last fall

we fall for all of this.

Gobtobler

is what we called it

when nicknaming months
made months the kind of
bearable

they're really just not.

Gobtobler

just the month you moved in
the first & latest

of months both too long
and not the fun they

used to/should be.

The mall is filled
with masked up zombies

shambling around stores
hopelessly filled with sanitizers

in hopes that emaciated, zombie
fingers

finger fondling every piece of
clothing

strewn atop forgot-how-to-stock
shelves

does enough in the way of
combating inevitable fourth waves

to make shopping for This Fall's

Must Have Top!

anything other than

the outright masturbatory exercise
in futility

returning to shopping in malls
ever again

already is.

Every post-apocalyptic movie on Netflix, ever

told us this was coming

In lieu of blindly leaping
into the oblivion of inevitability,

I'm happy the couch I watched this
all coming from

was the couch I shared with you.

Passports

aren't just tickets to exotic places now

and the restrictions

we're admittedly used to be restricted to

are as commonplace as the distrust
they tend to produce

but I'll produce mine,
this passport decidedly less fun

than the aforementioned kind

if it means I can access
places to purchase produce

and sink further into a beautifully
foolish dream

that this isn't reality and the rest of

my somber little semi-life.

AMIDST
AN EVER INCREASING
SERIES OF
INCREASINGLY SERIOUS
RESTRICTIONS AND REGULATIONS
YOU'RE
THE ONE THING
THAT MAKES THE REST OF
THESE ENTIRELY NONSENSICAL
EVERYTHINGS
MAKE SOMETHING SEMI CLOSE
TO SENSE.

You know it's getting bad

when Tammy, my injection specialist

and

Delores, my injection specialist

are two of the most important-significant characters

in this little book;

guess I don't get out as much as I maybe used to

and guess I'm maybe used to
a world where met-you-once injection specialists

are among the more significant interactions

a man can make
in the course of a really shitty half-year.

I'm in the throes
of self-imposed
makeshift miseries
and the woes
that inevitably come
with mid-life make-believes

when here you come,
perpetual high-pony
and the kind of
'married' that makes
chasing
worth something
stronger than whiskey I chase
to muster the strength to.

Black Ink
White Paper

because the colors ran
out of my worldview
and American spelling
and just Grey

all that's left
right or not

no matter what spellchecks
or concerned parents
say

all I'm left with
is all You left.

Here's to Skullduggery

&

Sadness.

I'm thinking about the walks
And the talks that inevitably came
with

(--and not just because that shit
rhymes)

You know I was always a better poet
than that

But not enough of one
To scare you into staying

Like fear of the (also inevitable)
Tell-All

We both knew I'd eventually have to
publish

Told you like the talks on those
walks

That talking you into sticking
around

Wasn't something you're thinking
back on

And thinking maybe you should have

You look at me
with eyes that don't make sense
and
maybe shouldn't

Looking at me
is precursor to the knowing me
that gnaws at you
long after lingering looks
fade into abject indignation

Call me

after you read this

i'll color all the commentary

you pretend you don't comprehend.

For what it's worth
I read all the great books
to make a great man

The Prince
couldn't fix me
&
Thoughts or Meditations
didn't land the way Marcus maybe hoped
&
while
The 120 Days of Sodom
was fun, the Marquis came closest
but couldn't

save

one scared little boy
from deep-rooted feelings of

feeling not so great.

"I'M GETTING RID OF THE PARTS I WROTE
WHEN I WAS DRUNK"

MEANS

QUARANTINE CONFESSIONS 2

IS

2 PAGES

&

ONLY

&

1 OF THOSE

IS THE TITLE PAGE.

It's
National Boyfriend Day

because that's a thing
&
the thing of it is

I used to be boyfriend
material
&
now
the nation that reads this

is really thankful I'm not

small town boy

medium town ambitions

and while I didn't / have not

conquered the world
we find ourselves in

13 books and
the groupies that follow

distract me from
the more glaring of failures

I find myself

familiarly failing.

It rains

a little much for my liking

fall falling a little fast

for my liking

&

temperament suitings alone,

I'd rather leaves take time in their collective leavings,

&

me to

the mirth that comes

with rapidly falling rains

&

rapidly turning leaves.

FOR
A GUY WHO SPENT
HIS BEST YEARS
PUTTING TRUTHS TO PAPER

THE TRUTH IS
YOURS IS THE ONE STORY
I'D LIKE TO KEEP
ALL TO MYSELF.

YOU'RE ALL

HIGH PONY

HIGH SOCKS

AND THE EFFECT ON ME

IS AFFECTING MY RELATIVELY SELFISH

ABILITY TO BE WALLOWING IN MISERY

THE LENGTH OF THOSE LEGS

AND THE HEIGHT OF YOUR HAIR

HAS ME COMMITTING BAD IDEAS TO PAPER

AND RELEGATING BAD INTENTIONS

TO THE DARK PLACES

PREVIOUSLY FILLED WITH

WHAT HAS TURNED OUT TO BE

ATTRACTIVE SELF-DESTRUCTIVENESS

SELF-DESTRUCTIVENESS
I'M HAPPY TO SHARE WITH YOU
AND THOSE RIDICULOUSLY
LONG LEGS.

Go on,

tell me I'm no good

I'm only on Page 125

of the 200 I need

to sell this book &

save this soul &

seal this damn

dam &

patch this hole

YOU'LL HAVE TO EXCUSE ME

BUT YOU AND THOSE

DON'T MAKE ANY KIND OF SENSE EYES

HAVE LEFT ME OUT OF THE KIND OF WORDS

I NORMALLY RESERVE

TO OUTLINE

THE MISTAKES

YOU'RE ABOUT TO MAKE.

Equal parts

scared little boy

&

tortured artist

&

semi-well-intentioned

interested party.

You still hurt more
than stubbed toes & skinned
knees

bad reviews & unrecognized
greatness

so congrats

you own the place
the pieces go to hide

bruised & bloodied & somehow
still

waiting for you to pick them up

& discard them all over again.

HAD THE LAST OF
THE LAST BATCH OF COOKIES
YOU BAKED BEFORE
YOU SAID GOODBYE.

AND, TO BE HONEST, THEY WERE THE KIND OF
BITTER

MY METAPHORICALLY INCLINED MIND MUST
SAY

SAYING GOODBYE TOOK THE SWEET
OUT OF THAT PARTICULAR BRAND
OF PARTICULARLY SUGARY TREAT

AND SO THE COOKIES ARE GONE

TOO

AND I'M LEFT TO CLEAN UP
THE CRUMBS OF YOU.

I'm good with words
but not good enough
to keep Red-haired her
or blonde-haired her
(or blonde-haired her)
or black-haired her
(and that one, in particular and
particularly hurt)

So forgive me
if Brown-haired You
is met with cautionary tales
and the kind of trepidation
that prefers you are kind,

in your judgments of me
and
the words misspelled on purpose
and
in efforts to keep you.

THAT GYPSY TOLD ME
YEAH, I'M GOOD AND CURSED
AND FUCKING GLOBAL PANDEMICS ASIDE
MY LUCK'S BEEN PRETTY GOOD

IF YOU COUNT
LOSING THE LATEST
IN A LAUNDRY LIST OF
ADMITTEDLY EPIC LOSSES
I'VE BEEN LOSING SINCE

THAT FIGHT WITH JOHNNY REIMER

MY KEYS

YOU.

Big fan of

your eyes & that ass &

the things about you that
don't make sense

eyes & ass aside

things like the way you
bother with me

the way

the way I am doesn't seem to
bother you

the way it so clearly
bothered

every-all of the rest of
them

without those eyes & that
ass

the way they all
unfortunately are

also without me

your biggest, latest fan

& of the way you won't leave

the way they couldn't wait
to.

I'm on a date

and, aside from the oddities associated

with showing two pieces of government-issued ID

and

two pdf documents documenting my double dose

the rest of this,

first date Friday

is about as close to normal

as an emotionally destroyed

semi-talented documentarian/writer can hope for;

and

so it's You

and

those eyes

and

that ass

and

this,

our first-last
semi-desperate attempt

at some fleeting form
of good-intentioned normalcy.

The line at the grocery store
is playing tricks on me
like we're almost out of this
mess we collectively find
ourselves in,

like there's light at the end
of this maybe-never-ending
checkout line,

hope for the lost souls like
me
and Hungry-Man dinner Fred,

in line & equally

& equally in this mess

& this line

& judging by the look on his
Hungry-Man face,

about the only guy in this
mess

& this line

maybe more miserable than me.

No marriage.

No kids.

No hope.

...right?

Blame Covid
for the rampant
pining these 139 pages or so
produce.
and I shop for my own now
masked up and hiding
the emotions I reserve
for grocery shopping
and writing
the really sad shit I write
because I have to
(fucking grocery shop.)

NO
SUCH
ANIMAL
IN
THE
WILD.

Sitting across tables

and over what might be really fucking good salmon

and the i can't tell is less because i'm not eating

and more because it's been seven years

since i've sat across tables

and stared into eyes

that burned for seven

with the kind of

'fuck you'

that swore i'd never have the opportunity

to sit across tables again.

I really don't remember
my dog Dabber

but I'm relatively sure
I wrote about her
more than once,

so you're in good company,

poem #142,

and

likely not the last
I'll write in order to

Remember

All of the things I should probably
forget about you.

Here's a deep cut

--I'm that oiled-up guy
playing saxophone on the
beach at the beginning of
'LOST BOYS'

little out of place,
but makes sense in the grand
scheme of things,

all "fuck it, it's a movie
about vampires anyways."

TO BE FAIR,

I'M NOT EVEN SURE SPEED DIAL IS A THING ANYMORE

BUT IF YOU ONLY TAKE ONE THING FROM

THIS ADMITTEDLY EXHAUSTING, SELF-INDULGENT HAIL MARY FOR MENTAL HEALTH

--YOU'RE FIRMLY PRESET #1

If this pandemic
proves the death of me

let my cost-effective
tiny tombstone read

HERE LIES _____

HE BROKE EVERYTHING HE EVER TOUCHED

& HE YEARNED FOR THINGS HE NEVER COULD

HE NEVER REALLY SOLD A BOOK
OR CLIMBED A MOUNTAIN

BUT HE SURE LIKED YOU A LOT.

It's late and you're tired
and I'm tired too

so I'll keep this one brief
and talk less about you.

Ever wonder how you end up with
Tupperware?

Like maybe mine came from

Her

or

Her

or

Her

or

Her

or

Her

or

Her

or

her

or

Her;

Red lids

I know I'd never buy

Never match the clear plastic bowls
one of you was so clearly fond of

and it accumulates
in your collective wakes;
Red lid reminders
that you were here

once
and, apparently, long enough
to move in Tupperware.

so
apparently
getting sick
from jab one or jab two
is something
some people do

blame the cocaine or the
whiskey
or the cocaine and the
whiskey
for the way my body
eagerly accepts
even the most dubious of
doses

so
bring on the booster
because I'm here for it

microdosing more than the
psyllicibin the lockdown
has me experimenting with

in light of other
medically beneficial (?)
medicines coursing through

already poisoned veins.

You come around
about as often as Adele albums

five years removed and maybe past due
because I've been needing and needy
neatly folding not easily contained
memories of the things you did
and the things you do
and continue to

so it's
water under the bridge
or it's not

my memories are as fuzzy
as the pictures we took
way back when
iPhone cameras were forgiving
the way you're maybe not so much.

pain comma plenty.

THE WAY MY MIND WORKS
DOESN'T WORK

BUT YOU DON'T SEEM TO MIND
AND SO HERE'S TO BOOK 13
OF MODERATELY MEDICATED MUSINGS

AS TO THE NOT-SO-SUBTLE WAYS
I INTEND TO WIN YOU BACK.

PART THREE.

Poems for Not Falling Apart.
(In a Global Pandemic.)

I don't see the parallels
because parallels are for
parking

and the past, recent
regurgitates reasons

you and you, plural
left for greener pastures

amidst claims it wasn't me

when the parking indicators
indicate

it sure as fuck was.

I filled a notebook
and three years for this

so, excuse me if the
memories that come back
come back hard

maybe they'll last longer
than global pandemics
and this stint
wherever you ran off to
runs to

but in the meantime
you can have this,
the contents of a notebook
and three good years

Hope it's enough
to keep you warm
in the years to come

the years I'm gone
and you're left
with the memories my
notebook

makes you remember

everytime you face the
words

facing back at you.

GHOST MEDICINE

FOR MEDICATING THE MORE ABSTRACT
OF YOUR FREQUENT COMINGS
AND TIRED GOINGS.

You're distractingly pretty
as pretty distractions go

and I am

going

to spend the rest of
the less pretty words
I typically paint with

painting praises
better heaped upon you.

APOLOGIES

IF DATING ME

WAS SPENDING COMPANY

WITH THE GHOSTS OF THEM

THEY RARELY REST

AND WHISPER THE LESS WELL-INTENTIONED

OF ALREADY ADMITTEDLY SEMI-WELL-INTENTIONED

WORDS I WHISPERED

NO LESS LOUDLY

IN AND AMONGST

THE WHISPERED WORDS

THAT DROVE YOU IN DIRECTIONS

THAT WILL ONE DAY

LEAVE YOU

(LIKE YOU LEFT ME)

JUST A GHOST

IN MY HEAD

AND A LITTLE LESS

NO BETTER THAN THE REST OF THEM.

I miss

Pizza Hut's lunchtime buffet
a TV show called Banshee
and
my slightly-wasted thirties

I barely remember
my dog Dabber
and
the way the world worked
when masks were just on Halloween

but
one thing I don't miss
and sure as fuck remember

is the way you looked at me
the very first time
you knew you were in love
and
the way I thought
my days of writing sad books were done

turns out I was wrong

and so good luck with
the rest of your already-better life

I'll be here
barely remembering
and writing

really sad books
about why
it's better to forget.

Write volumes
so I don't speak them

perceived cowardice in
person

betrays avarice behind
eyes
spent scanning pages

for the right words to
write

all the volumes it will
inevitably take

to make this up to you.

REST

IS
A

FOUR-LETTER WORD

&
REALLY

AND

I'M JUST

REALLY, REALLY SAD
IT DIDN'T WORK OUT

&
THE REST THAT
COMES MEANS I'LL
GET NONE

BECAUSE

REST

IS
A
FOUR-LETTER WORD

&
REALLY.

LOVE

IS
A

FOUR-LETTER WORD

TOO

&

UNFORTUNATELY.

There's hope in those legs
to say nothing of those eyes
and that ass

hope in the way
there's been anything but
since the last set of legs
to box my ears

boxed my ears
more than metaphorically

so wrap those lengthy legs
around me and more than metaphorically
because I'm here for it

you

and the emotional entanglements
we make in the tangling.

You seem to have

an ability to take over

the totality of my thought
process

I mean. I used to reserve some
for
professionally necessary misery
and
the abject morbidity that comes
with creativity like mine

--and now it's pretty much you.

BADLY BROKEN BOYS DO IT BETTER.

YOU
SAY THAT ADULT LIFE MAKES IT HARDER

AND I TELL YOU IT'S THE WORST
AND I WOULD SAY FOR THE BEST
BUT I'M SELFISH AND LIFE IS SHORT

SO SEEING YOU STAYS A PRIORITY

RIGHT UP THERE WITH THE SELF-IMPOSED MISERY
IT TAKES TO WRITE THE KIND OF NOT-KIND WORDS I WRITE

AND RIGHT UP THERE WITH THE LIES I TELL MYSELF AND TO ASSURE ME I'M THE KIND OF CLEVER IT TAKES

TO COME UP WITH A WAY AROUND
THE SELF-IMPOSED WALLS
YOU'RE SO POORLY IMPOSING.

these talks go best
when it's impossibly late
&
impossible.

StAY

because I still need Jesus & a pretty big bath

but the sins I wash away

aren't half the story of the ones that StAY

the way your head tells you
you really, really shouldn't

but
that pull
in the pit of your tiny little stomach

tells you
you really, really should.

HONESTLY

...IS THIS SHIT AS EXHAUSTING TO YOU IN
THE READING

AS IT WAS TO ME IN THE WRITING?

Write for days

talk for hours

because the time it takes

to mend the wounds

I'm so hell-bent on wounding

means I need more than just the minutes

it took to fool you

to talk myself out of

the months of messes

you and those fat little lips

are moving to convince me

time

is something we have anywhere close

to enough of.

FIRST - TEAM
ALL ENERGY

I GET THE FEELING
THIS IS THE ONE THAT WILL BLOW UP
AFTER I'M DEAD

LIKE THEY'LL SAY

"THAT @brodydrew COULDN'T HOLD A DAMN RELATIONSHIP"

"OR MAKE ANYTHING OF HIMSELF WHEN HE WAS HERE"

"BUT FUCK, COULD THAT HANDSOME DEVIL TURN A PHRASE AND TWIST A TONGUE SILVER AND OTHERWISE"

WINDING WORDS AND CHURNING
FEELINGS IN PLACES
YOU ONLY FEEL
WHEN THE PERSON RESPONSIBLE FOR THE STORM

IS DEAD AND GONE AND

APPRECIATED LIKE THE SUN

AFTER SAID STORMING.

STILL

colder than your step-father

when it comes to this writing shit

and

daddy issues aside

I'll play roles
assigned only to places
your better judgment
goes to hide.

OF ALL THE EMOTIONS I COULD INSTILL

I'LL TAKE "TERRIFIED"

HAPPY TO INSTILL EMOTIONS, STRONG

OVER THE APATHY YOU SO CLEARLY SAVE

FOR THE ONES YOU MAYBE MEAN IT

WHEN YOU SAY

"love"

HERE'S TO HARSH FADES
&
HEAD SCARS.

SACCHARINE SADNESS

SWEET ENOUGH FOR YOUR MORNING COFFEE.

She says

"I have the most to lose"

and I'm like

"all due respect, it's

mind

clothes

aside

you're oh-so-safe with me."

OF ALL THE THINGS
I'M OUT TO DO TO YOU,

"HURT"

ISN'T ONE OF THEM.

NOT TO PUSH THE BOUNDARIES

JUST KNOW YOU CAN'T MOVE THE GOALPOSTS FAR ENOUGH TO BE OUT OF BOUNDS.

lionize me
/
idolize you.

AROUND HERE

GOBTOBLER 25TH

IS THE DAY THIS ALL OFFICIALLY ENDS,

WHILE MASKS MIGHT BE AROUND UNTIL MARCH

THE END OF
GOBTOBLER

SEES THE END OF THE RESTRICTIONS WE'VE BEEN OH-SO-RESTRICTED TO;

AND WHILE
GOBTOBLER
IS A PARTICULARLY SPOOKY SEASON--

　　　　　　　--IT NOW HAS REASONS
　　　　　　　　　　　　OTHER THAN

　　　　　　　　　　THE GHOSTS OF
　　　　　　　　　　　　GOBTOBLER
　　　　　　　　　　　　　　　PAST

TO CELEBRATE THE END

OF FEELINGS THAT FALL
LONGER THAN LINGERINGS

OF OVERSTAYED SICKNESS.

November

November

--can fuck right off

Gobtobler always spooky-long

and

lingering

like the ghost

you up and turned into.

November

for real this time

winter is coming

and

for any hope

I had prior to your goings

There's a formula for all of this;

meet her/love her/let her break you

let the pieces she leaves

leave you

set the scene amongst the horrors of
horribly oppressive globally-relatable
situations...

...fill this page, and the pages that
follow
with the kind of uncompromising rage
the pieces leave in their leaving,
too.
Or '2' because this is the sequel, latest
in a series of lamentations
directly related to the myriad reasons
why.

iT's aMazIng to mE

hoW the seconD parT of ThIS comes eAsier

thaN the firsT

like writing sad shit about the people you miss really tries to make you miss the people who could keep the sadness somewhere else.

November and the inevitable arrival of flu season

Practically guarantees Quarantine Confessions 3

like vaccinations comma billions

can keep the restrictions that constrict

us

the away we've all prayed/waited for

for at least as <u>long</u> as I've been putting

sad shit to paper,

way too

and longing for a flu season that is a

flu season and <u>just.</u>

I realize I'm running out of road

patience you have for writing like this
wearing as thin as the fabric of the
workout pants I prefer you
workout in
but(t) if you bear (bare) with me, I promise
more than immature ramblings designed
to fake a depth
you've seen through since
I noticed how good you really do look
in those thin fabric workout pants.

WE REALLY DO NEED
TO STOP FOR A SECOND
AND FIGURE OUT
THOSE FUCKING EYES

...THEY DON'T MAKE SENSE
AND I'M LOSING MINE
AND MORE THAN THE ONE
THAT CAUGHT MY ATTENTIONS
IN THE FIRST PLACE

LIKE NO EXPECTATION/OBLIGATION, BUT YOU ON MY COUCH FEELS LIKE AN INEVITABILITY

Fall
fell

a little too fast

into laps you left
me alone

falling faster
than leaves

from trees outside
inside voices & metaphors

for falling
out of love

the way you most
certainly

fell

this

Fall.

dreams, no fever.

No anxiety
Just indulgence

..because Google Maps tells me you're
exactly 200 kilometers away

and I'm nothing if not
wasted time and a full tank of gas.

SEEING YOU ON WEEKENDS IS SOMETHING
SEEING YOU ON ONE WEEKEND
MADE ME SPOILED TO.

SO I'M IN THIS RESTAURANT
HAVING SHOWN VACCINE
PASSPORTS

AND

APPROPRIATELY PHOTOGENIC
REPRESENTATIONS ON PHOTO ID

WHEN THE NEWS BREAKS
THAT ALL THIS IS OVER

AND

THE CAPACITY LIMITS WE'RE
COLLECTIVELY **OBEYING/
IGNORING**

CAN LOSE THE WORD BEFORE
/IGNORING,

*and I'm not

IGNORING

THE LOOK IN YOUR EYES

EYES THAT DON'T **MAKE SENSE**
AND YET

SOMEHOW,

WITH ANNOUNCEMENTS LIKE THE
ONE JUST ANNOUNCED

TELL US AT LEAST SOMETHING IS

STARTING TO.

fuck these masks

while they make those eyes pop

those eyes that don't make sense

they at least make the kind of sense

that tells me

looking at the rest of that resplendent little face

is better for quelling

the ocean of anxiety

that gazes back at me

from the table we wait to be
seated at

for the remainder of the
revealing.

feel like you're hours and hours worth of
conversation.

and exploration.

my list of amusing muses
aren't always amused
by the ones they figure
aren't about them;

and so you've got them all on their
collective toes

tipping
and
trying

to discern the length of
your pretty long
pretty little legs

and

you've got them collectively hoping
the height of their high ponys

collectively touches
the really high height of
your high fucking pony.

This one is fat
like your fat little ass

the way you barely fit
into those tights you barely fit
into

has me,
into you and

this fat little volume
that I'm about to finish

so you can be more to me
than the reason I picked up the pen

again

and to finish it.

petty as fuck
but you're here for it.

pretty as fuck
and I'm here for it.

COME OVER
AND LEAVE THE BAGGAGE
WHERE THE BAGGAGE IS BETTER OFF

BACK HOME AND WONDERING
WHERE THE LOVE OF HIS LIFE, TOO

UP AND RAN OFF TO

LOST LIKE THAT SOCK
FROM THE LAUNDRY YOU LEFT
HIM TO

TOO

ON YOUR WAY OUT THE DOOR
AND
MOTHERFUCKING

MORE THAN METAPHORICALLY.

LET'S BE HONEST
THAT MAN YOU WENT OFF
AND MARRIED
IS BETTER FOR 99 REASONS

99 REASONS AND THEY'RE
ALL
RIGHT

99 REASONS, SAVE
1

YOU'RE HERE RIGHT NOW
WITH ME

THE WAY YOU NEVER
REALLY
LEFT.

...

WAIT, BEFORE YOU GET MAD
ABOUT THAT 99 REASONS
SHIT,

REMEMBER THE POEM ABOUT
THAT MAN YOU WENT OFF
AND MARRIED

COULD BE ABOUT YOU
OR
YOU
OR
YOU
OR
YOU
OR
YOU,

YOU ALL PREFER PATTERNS
AND,
DESPITE SAID 99 REASONS
I'M THE
1
YOU ALL HAVE IN COMMON,

COLD COMFORT FOR LOVING

THE LOST THINGS
YOU ALL SO COMMONLY
LOVE.

don't go

stay

don't go

stay

don't go

stay

don't go

stay

don't go

stay

i broke you
like that toy

you broke me
like that boy

i guess i never really stopped being

scared and too

and

entirely too afraid
to face up to

breaking the tiny pretty things

boys like me
always seem to break.

...

(late)

NOVEMBER.

FORGIVE ME
BUT FOR A GUY WHO SPENDS HIS FRIDAYS
GETTING PUNCHED IN THE FACE

IM HERE FOR ANY METAPHORICAL BEATINGS
YOU AND YOUR TOO RAPIDLY BEATING HEART
ARE ENTHUSIASTICALLY MOVING
RAPIDLY PARTING LIPS

TO MORE THAN METAPHORICALLY BEAT ME.

When working on it

isn't working out

I'm both viable option/inevitable conclusion

wrapped up in one pretty, pretty much more than a little self-destructive package.

After all of this whining/introspection/self-destruction/reflection/misery...

...it looks like there might be light at the end of this proverbial tunnel, pandemically (is that a word?) speaking, so bye.

ANXIETY ACCELERATING
SURE

BUT I'M ALL
MARVIN'S ROOM ON REPEAT

JUST SAYING YOU COULD DO BETTER

AND I'LL START HATING ONLY IF YOU
MAKE ME

ABOUT THE ONLY LINES I'LL BORROW

FAR FROM

THE ONLY LINES I'LL CROSS

SO I UNDERSTAND THE HEART RACING
LESS SO THE MIND

BECAUSE YOU MADE UP YOURS
LONG BEFORE THAT FIRST TIME

YOU DROVE ALL THE WAY OVER

OVER

ANOTHER GOOD DRAKE SONG
BUT ONE WE CAN'T RELATE TO.

SMILE,

YOU'RE STILL THE ONLY ONE IN THE WHOLE WORLD

WHO KNOWS MY FAVORITE FOUR LETTER WORD.

240 Pages of Forward.

162, 2.

BECAUSE OVERTHINK ABOUT YOU IS ALL I DO.

Our Chemicals don't play nice.

QUARANTINE

CONFESSIONS

3

aka
(for better or worse)

The Ballad of Billy Ancaster

BILLY BLOWS IT

is the ending to this one,

but I figured I'd do it different

because we're in month comma who-cares

of a pandemic that won't end

and no one wants to read about cases

and chronology

and since formatting was never really a forté

I'm going in directions decidedly different

telling same stories in new ways

and this one

is about how Billy A

burned it down with YOU.

PART ONE

Introducing

Billy Aucaster

Bold

Brave

Bashful,

Billy Ancaster is one of those

not-particularly-good-at-anything kind of protagonists,

though he fancies himself a pugilist and a poet,

and so understanding the particularly twisted kind of psychology that produces either of those professions is for your particular consideration

--imagine the twisted fuck who fancies himself both?

...

To make matters worse,

Billy Ancaster is aging the kind of rapidly we collectively realize

just a little too late,

and so the road ahead

--a road filled with what he hopes are the attentions of the beautiful (always seemingly ortherwise-committed) women

is maybe a little shorter in distance
than the admittedly impressive/horrifying

litter of hearts and corresponding bodies

he left lying

on the road behind.

The Covid 19 pandemic,

now in Year Three

isn't helping

the not-so-quiet desperation

our Brave Billy is feeling,

and the most recent rebuking
of his most recent love,

and the immediately following and
equally awful

rebuking of the one right after,

have left Billy despondent and

maybe a little pissed,

and at the every-other girl

foolish enough to become
emotionally entangled with him

victims of the poetry on every page

that follows this one.

Let me tell you a little about

BILLY FUCKING ANCASTER

Billy Ancaster has a hole in his head.
(It's real, and it's on the cover of this
book.)

It's shaped like a heart, which is both fun
and maybe a little accurate,

because maybe there's a hole in his heart,
too.

And so one is frighteningly real
(--and not just because I'm really Billy
and that hole is really fucking scary)

and one is at least metaphorically real

and both matter because

both inform

the mistakes I made about you,

and the reason Billy

gets a book about him.

Billy

has a brother named **Johnny**

and Johnny Ancaster is a big part of this book.

Johnny Ancaster has a bit of a temper,

so keep that in mind,

but Johnny cares about his brother

--and is full of semi-well-intentioned good advice

so Billy takes his advice
in ways he really maybe only sometimes should.

Because Johnny is basically a pitbull
some deity shaved and pretended to pass as human

and so his worldview is restricted to
the kinds of things pitbulls pretending as
humans can't pretend to care about

chasing tail and eating raw and not
suffering fools or lesser canines

--things to keep in mind when considering
the perspectives supplied by

Johnny Fucking Ancaster.

A LITTLE MORE ABOUT BILLY A.

BILLY WAS BORN IN THE MUD AND THE SUMMER

AND BOTH ARE REASONS

BILLY GETS A BOOK.

BECAUSE THE MUD MADE HIM ANGRY,

COMING THE WAY HE DID AND FROM ABSOLUTELY NOTHING MORE.

AND THE SUMMER MADE HIM SELFISH,

ASTROLOGY CROWNING HIM LION AND THEREFORE KING.

SO BILLY WAS A MESS

LONG BEFORE THE LOOKS
-HE WILL SO HUMBLY POINT OUT-

THAT LET HIM GET AWAY WITH IT,

ANGRY AND SELFISH AND UNLEASHED

UPON PRETTY GIRLS WHO SHOULD HAVE KNOWN BETTER,

PRETTY GIRLS JUST LIKE

YOU.

nature **VS** nurture

...and it wasn't even close.

(brave)

BILLY ANCASTER &

The Thing About Fridays.

Billy Ancaster spends his Friday nights

getting punched in the face

hard,

because Billy Ancaster fashions himself a boxer,

and because boxers do nothing if not box.

So Fridays end bloody

and Fridays end bruised

because the guy Billy boxes

is named Tyson (—really!)

and Ten-Round Tyson's got fifty pounds
on Billy easy,

and so Friday Night Fights are anything
but,

Billy working out as-advertised and
constantly-surfacing demons

hoping repeated head trauma

quiets the more restless

of voices whispering

in still-ringing ears.

JOHNNY ANCASTER

loves weed

like BILLY ANCASTER

loves unavailable women. *

So lots,

and the rest of this book

is about the litany of mistakes made

under the influence

&

in service of

addictions both chosen

and wonderfully unavoidable.

Unavailable woman *

Careful putting prettily
manicured fingers through
proverbial and poorly-tethered
cages.

Late nights

are

for whiskey

and

fever dreams

and

the everything else I do

to fail at forgetting

you.

Billy Ancaster

is at the age

where life starts taking

the pop on his jab

his Aunt Lou

his first and favorite dog

and you

and you

and you

and you

and you

latest and last of the ones smart

enough to leave him

while he was good looking enough

to get away with it.

PART TWO

Big Red.

BIG RED
IS ANYTHING BUT,

ALL OF ONE HUNDRED AND
FIVE POUNDS

OF THE KIND OF PRETTY

THAT MAKES HER

A BIG FUCKING DEAL

FOR BOTH BILLY ANCASTER
AND THE REST OF THIS BOOK

BECAUSE HER UP AND LEAVING
HIM

AFTER THREE-AND-A-HALF
OF THE BEST YEARS OF HIS
LIFE

HAS LEFT HIM

ON THE KIND OF RAMPAGE

THAT WILL HAVE ALL OF THE
GIRLS

AFTER BIG RED

READING THIS BETWEEN THE FINGERS

COVERING THEIR PRETTY-AS-WELL EYES

AND NO LONGER WONDERING

JUST WHAT IN THE HELL

GOT INTO HIM

TO MAKE BRAVE BILLY ANCASTER

TAKE IT OUT ON EACH AND EVERY ALL OF THEM

HOW WE GOT IN THIS MESS

BRAVE BILLY ANCASTER COMES HOME
BRAVELY
SOME MONDAY NIGHT AFTER WORK.

IT'S LATE, BECAUSE WORK GOES LATE—LATE
ENOUGH TO BE DARK OUTSIDE, DARK ON SOME
LATE SUMMER DAY.

BRAVE BILLY COMES HOME, AND—MAYBE ODE
TO HIS FORTHCOMING MISFORTUNE—
DOESN'T NOTICE IT'S UNUSUALLY DARK IN
HIS APARTMENT, AS WELL.

THERE'S A GIRL ON HIS ADMITTEDLY
EXPENSIVE COUCH,
WHICH ISN'T UNUSUAL,
TONIGHT (OR ANY OTHER, TO BE FAIR TO THE
APPEAL OF BRAVE BILLY)
AND IT'S NOT UNUSUAL TONIGHT,
BECAUSE

THE GIRL IS BIG RED,
AND BIG RED IS HIS GIRLFRIEND.

BIG RED IS SITTING IN THE DARK
AND BEFORE THE FIRST FLICK OF THE LIGHT
SWITCH
BRAVE BILLY CAN'T HELP BUT NOTICE
HOW HER EYES SEEM TO BE GLOWING,

GLOWING A LOT LIKE A RACCOON'S EYES SEEM
TO GLOW, RIGHT AFTER GETTING CAUGHT
WITH THEIR CUTE LITTLE PAWS GOING
THROUGH YOUR GARBAGE.

BRAVE BILLY FLICKS THE LIGHT SWITCH,
AND—QUICKER THAN THE ROOM CAN LIGHT
UP—BEGINS REGALING BIG RED WITH BIG
USELESS RECOUNTINGS OF THE COMPLETELY
MEANINGLESS EVENTS OF HIS BIG
INCONSEQUENTIAL DAY.

BRAVE BILLY FAILS TO NOTICE,
SOMEWHAT TRAGICALLY,
THAT THE WILD IN BIG RED'S EYES
HASN'T DISSIPATED WITH THE LIGHTING OF
THE ROOM AROUND HER.

NOW
BIG RED
IS REALLY LITTLE LILI,
BECAUSE THAT'S REALLY HER REAL NAME

BUT REGARDLESS OF WHAT HE CHOOSES TO
CALL HER, LITTLE LILI LISTENS POLITELY

THE WAY SHE HAS LISTENED POLITELY
TO THE RANTINGS OF BRAVE BILLY
FOR ALMOST FOUR YEARS.

WHEN HE'S DONE,
DONE WAILING ABOUT THE INCONSEQUENTIAL
EVENTS OF HIS INCONSEQUENTIAL DAY,
SHE POLITELY PARTS THE LIPS

ON HER PRETTY LITTLE FACE

AND TELLS HIM

IN EQUALLY PRETTY TONES AND WITH
MODESTLY CHOSEN WORDS

THAT SHE'S LEAVING HIM

IMMEDIATELY

AND TO MOVE THOUSANDS AND THOUSANDS OF
MILES

AWAY.

HE CAN'T COME
AND
SHE'S QUIT THE JOB
SHE HAD WORKING
AT THE SAME PLACE
AS BRAVE BILLY
ALREADY

AND

WHILE SHE WOULD VERY MUCH LIKE
TO LIVE WITH POOR BRAVE BILLY
FOR THE TWO WEEKS IT WILL TAKE

FOR HER TO BE READY TO UP AND LEAVE HIM,
FOR REAL,

SHE WOULD CERTAINLY UNDERSTAND
IF SHE COULD NOT.

HE LETS HER,
STAY

BECAUSE HE LOVES HER

AND WHEN THE TWO WEEKS ARE
UNMERCIFULLY
GONE

SO IS SHE,
BIG RED
OR
LITTLE LILI

LEAVES HIM
TO THE PROBABLY-BETTER LIFE
SOMEWHERE OUT WEST
HE JUST WASN'T LOVED ENOUGH
TO BE BROUGHT TO, TOO.

...

*PLUS, SHE LEAVES HIM IN THE MIDDLE OF A PANDEMIC.

NO WONDER EVERYONE ELSE IN THIS BOOK IS FUCKED.

I'd say
I put my heart in it

but we both know
you took that

like that mug you know I loved,

cold comforts and coffee
all I'm left with

and the lack of warmth
heart
and
caffeinated thoughts

make Quarantine Confessions 3

your fault
and for more than
the oh-so-painfully obvious.

...

SO THERE YOU HAVE IT.

BRAVE BILLY ANCASTER

SPENDS THE REST OF THIS BOOK

GETTING PUNCHED IN HIS STUPID PRETTY FACE,

AND NOW YOU KNOW WHY.

...

Big Red is gone
and he misses her,

and he takes her leaving

like a left from Ten-Round Tyson

first crack

in an already

slowly-cracking skull.

...

BIG RED REACHES OUT
FROM THE TOP OF
THE FUCKING MOUNTAIN
(LITERALLY)
HE MADE HER RUN AWAY
TO,
AND IN THE REACHING
REMINDS BRAVE BILLY
HOW MUCH OF HIMSELF
WAS LOST
ON THE DAY SHE
DROVE DIRECTIONS
PROMISING BEAUTIFUL VIEWS
AND
ANYTHING OTHER
THAN
FOOLISHLY PHONY
BRAVE LITTLE BOYS.

She says

"You're mine Billy Ancaster"

and it hurts

because it's true

and it hurts

because it took her

moving 2,000 miles

away

to stake a claim

she never had to.

BIG RED
's got someone ghostwriting her DM's
but Brave Billy isn't scared

he's been on some medium shit
seeing ghosts
since way back in '84

See, his chest Stays-Puft
Not the Marshmallow Man she figured
when she pulled the latest
scheme
on her steady-scheming shit.

*It might be the repeated blows to the head

that make bold Billy question
the admittedly-questionably typed
messages from Big Red/Little Lili,

but

synapses both firing and missing

have him missing her

and rationalizing leavings

as betrayals

because

it's all he understands,

and because

it's the only language he speaks.

...

Billy goes bad
is the next part of this book,

somewhat logically...

...because bad things happen to Billy
and
as the back of this book will tell you,

Billy is just a sad, scared little boy.

So when bad things happen to
bad Billy,

you can bet your bottom dollar

bad things happen to
everyone around him

because, and maybe just.

PART THREE

Doomed.

This is the first
of the ones about
the one right after,

the rest of which
make about as much sense

as both her eyes
and their attempts at
something supposedly close to
courtship,

rest assured
our Brave Billy
burns it down

with this one
the way he tends to,

concussions and consternations

about all he's good for

and about all he's got left.

...

Same animals

bare teeth

never

bow heads

It starts slow,
this next thing
& on the heels of the last multi-year
disappointment,

like maybe her
up & leaving
left Billy Ancaster the kind of
vulnerable
that allowed you
to go from casual possibility
to doomed eventuality.

So it starts slow,
all selfies and all-the-time-
conversation,
picking up steam and
not so slowly
hurtling towards the eventuality that
will see
you
up and leave
Billy Ancaster,
too.

...

forward

I'm told these conversations are best
when waged with carefully chosen and
clearly-stated words;

and I'm sorry

but we both know

I prefer riddles and intentions relegated
just under surfaces

better unsurfaced

when it comes to aggressive eye contact
and the words you want to follow

I'd argue don't need to

and you'd argue

that arguing is more of what
these pretense-laden
conversations
inevitably descend to

because for a guy supposedly good
with words

when it comes to bravery in the face
of

that pretty fucking face of yours

I'm two left feet and left without
the words it would take

to converse civilly and convince
you otherwise.

Billy Ancaster

lost his mind mid-September.

He'd known her for years,

this reason for mid-September madness,

all perpetually blue eyes

and the kind of body that complimented her pretty in ways that boys like Billy Ancaster almost always fall for.

He'd known her for years,

but mid-September is when she engaged in the kind of conversations that only ever end one way,

when it comes to Billy A.

She said she wasn't happy in her marriage

said so without expressly saying so

words sweet like the whatever-the-fuck she sipped on,

sitting on his expensive couch and sipping her expensive coffee and telling him the kinds of things she told him that first time she came over.

That first time would be the last time, but Billy couldn't possibly have known that, looking into her perpetually blue/green eyes and getting himself the in-over-his-head he tends to,

sometime just before this conversation ended in his bed.

...

But first,
energy.

THESE STORIES
DON'T END PRETTY

AND I LOSE EVERY FIGHT
I'VE EVER FOUGHT

BUT YOUR EYES DON'T MAKE SENSE

AND MY WILLINGNESS TO PICK MYSELF
UP OFF THE CANVAS
YOU PUT ME ON

MIGHT NOT EITHER,

BUT YOU'RE WORTH
AT LEAST TEN ROUNDS
AND THE HIT
BOTH MY RECORD AND
MY INFINITELY FRAGILE EGO

ARE ABOUT TO TAKE.

SO I GUESS WHAT
I'M SAYING IS

COME ON

TAKE WHAT YOU WANT

WHAT'S ONE MORE BUSTED LIP

TO A BARELY TETHERED HEART.

....

Best guess
she broke him
that first time she came over,

sometime between his rubbing her low
back on the balcony
and
the feeling he felt the first time she
rested her weary head on his chest.

She would regress
immediately after,

well, sometime between her drive home
and
whatever happened with her husband when
she got there,

but by the time he noticed
his heart was in it

the way his heart hadn't been in it
since Big Red.

Billy hated regression
the way Billy kinda hated everything
the morning after she was gone,

and that was before
he realized that
for good
was the kind of gone
she really was

maybe moments after he let her drive
home.

The concussions
--more accurately, the
trauma

have one beautiful benefit
for forlorn Billy Ancaster

--he only remembers
the good
band-aids the bad
and can't help but wonder
why she
takes her time
before responding
to his always ill-timed and worse-taken
invitations into
the vacuum that is
his orbit.

Your neck of the woods
because you're not local
but
you're not available, either
and that's never stopped us before.

And you can blame
your oft-referenced crippling anxiety
for reasons you won't
come out of the house
you supposedly no longer share

I'm here and waiting
maybe less than patiently
for you to realize
isolation
is better spent
anywhere but the

alone

you're so intent on imposing.

She struggles
and with more than her mental
and for far longer
than Bold Billy
and his
"let me fuck with your mental"
leanings,

so when she
doesn't look at him
with eyes that don't make sense

--and because she lives too far away to
come over

telling him

"I want to work on my marriage, I hope you understand"

he handles it
about as well as you'd imagine
and he

begins to unravel
at seams that were really never raveled

understanding nothing
despite assurances otherwise

and although
her marriage
is the kind of over
she was last weekend,

we all know
Bold Billy

won't hang around patiently
to pick up

the inevitable pretty pieces.

ALL DUE RESPECT
BUT

I KNEW YOU FIRST

AND
I LIKE(d) YOU MORE.

LOYALTY B(L)INDS.

He falls in love with the next one
well before he has any right to,

maybe because he loves her
maybe because he loves *her*

and either way
because
the whole wide world can't burn fast
enough

to make up for the hurt they've
collectively caused him.

Brash Billy Ancaster
good out the gate,
not so good
at the gates/cages
being good out of
eventually find him
painfully/terribly
trapped in.

SHE'S PULLING AWAY
AND
IN SO DOING
WINNING THE PROVERBIAL FIGHT
EVERY SINGLE ENTANGLEMENT
SORT OF IS,

AND
IF THERE'S ONE THING BILLY ANCASTER
HATES
IT'S LOSING ROUNDS

TO OPPOSITION HE'S CONFIDENT HE CAN
HANDLE

AND
HE CAN'T
HANDLE
ANYTHING REMOTELY RESEMBLING
THE REGRESSION

SHE'S SET ON REGRESSING TO,
THROWING WORDS

AND
WITH LESS FREQUENCY
THAN HE'S USED TO

AND
HE'S FRUSTRATED AND MOST LIKELY
CONCUSSED

AND SO
IT'S

A MESSAGE TO HER
IN THE DARK AND DESPERATION
AND THROWING THE ONE WORD

NO SELF-RESPECTING ROMEO
EVERY REALLY SHOULD.

Brave Billy
insofar as
he says the words
eyes do
but
pretty lips
won't painfully
part to.

NOTHING HURTS

LIKE WELL-TIMED LEFT HOOKS

AND

HEARING "NO THANK YOU"

IN RESPONSE TO

POORLY-TIMED

"I LOVE YOUS"

-billy ancaster.

*didn't mention that

poorly-timed "I love yous" were really confused feelings

masquerading as Hail Marys

for the head trauma induced

and really poorly-timed words

that led to the need for Hail Marys, at all.

Twisting tongues and feelings

trying to rationalize

situations that are anything but.

"I LOVE YOU"

is a mistake

always, and especially first

first signal
that you're waving white flags

and signaling
the loss of the only war
even remotely worth
fighting

the jockeying for
position, pole
in the battle to

at once

lose yourself and retain
that last little piece of
the dignity a

clearly spoken

"I LOVE YOU"

proves you maybe never had

if not most certainly just lost.

It was your eyes
that got us into this
mess,
but I can't fault you
for that.

It's my
fault
maybe calling you mine
before I had anything
remotely
close to the right to

and I was wrong
but not about the
wanting you
the way I really,
really
wanted you.

No
I was wrong
for maybe believing a
guy like me
deserved anything close
to
the way those eyes fell
on me
hoping maybe you'd
fall,

too.

Mr. Melancholy.

no offense, but the opp

(--and I don't mean your husband)

looks about five-six

and the kind of gassed-up

that makes making my age

the impossibility

we're turning out to be.

_ _ _ _ _ aka

"Doomed"

 is gone
and he misses her,

and he takes her leaving

like another left from Ten-Round Tyson

latest crack

coming decidedly close to

the last crack,

too many

too soon

for a

not so slowly-cracking skull.

...

BROKEN BILLY ANCASTER
CAN'T HELP BUT WONDER

WHAT'S WITH THESE BITCHES
UP AND DRIVING AWAY ON HIM

all these

months

and all these miles

and the bitch of it is

we both know I'm

still

simply ten digits and

one full tank away.

get over it

the tiny voice in the back of his still-
aching head said,

but the tiny voice is the same
one that told him
and on more than one occasion

don't get punched in the face
don't listen to Johnny Ancaster
let that kick in the balls from Johnny
Reimer go, it was twenty-nine years ago

and he hadn't bothered
with any of that

so the odds
of bold Billy Ancaster
getting over you

are about as likely
as the listening to reason
he hasn't done/won't do
since the tiny voice in the back of his
pretty-much-always aching head

suggested the first of the
semi-well-intentioned good ideas
long before the balls that would
inevitably be kicked

dropped

far too many better-yet-not-ignored
impulses ago.

...

IYKYK

Miss more
than your eyes
and that ass

and you blame me for
books written about both

but neither make sense

-what about us does tho

all false starts and fumbles
gnashed teeth and
terrible and terribly misinterpreted
words

trying to find
ways to say
words we really don't need to

words like

miss

and more than
the things we've established

I really do.

"You're not who I thought you were"

well,
You're not who I thought you were, either
and
your poorly disguised/easily translated
subtle little selfies
don't hit the same
and
you can blame the lighting
or the lack of open gyms,

either way
me and Drake will be over here
getting over you not so quietly
all Marvin's Room cranked on speakers
next to couches
I barely remember you curling up on.

...

Blame the
nothing-we-can-do-about-it
hole

in Brave Billy's
beautiful little head,

but the fucks he used to give
are decidedly less,

and so he's coming
quite frankly
for anyone who's hurt him
and the list is long
and his way with words hasn't waned
the way his memory
is trying to,

and so Quarantine Confessions 3
is The Ballad of Billy Ancaster
and a race to
remember
everyone who needs appropriate
rememberings

here on the path of his
war waged for revenge.

Poor
Billy Ancaster
lost his mind mid-September
broke his nose sometime after
broke his heart
a little too close
to the losing of things
that preceded the
swiftly transpiring
& ultimately inevitable
slew of breakings.

PART FOUR

Johnny Fucking Aucaster.

Johnny Ancaster

is into the weed again.

The weed & his feelings,

if and only because the two are anything but mutually exclusive.

And you'd be surprised to learn that shaved-down, pass-as-human pitbulls

feel things like feelings,

but Johnny Ancaster

is into the weed again,

and so here come the first of many insightful and longing-fueled feelings.

"You know"
says Johnny Ancaster
"the trouble with the women we tend to attract/fall for"

before continuing & between hits of rapidly disappearing blunts

Johnny Ancaster pauses for dramatic effect

if and only because Johnny Ancaster is nothing if not

a little dramatic.

"The trouble with the women"

--and I'll spare you the rest,
because the rest

is what the rest

of this whole goddamn book

is all about.

...

Getting involved
with an Ancaster
is equivalent
--more or less
--to
mainlining heroin
and sitting
through
Sunday service
at your local
place of worship

like the good
is really good
but kinda comes nowhere close
to scrubbing
the sins
it took
to sit that pretty ass
in that fucking pew.
...

So

BILLY ANCASTER

tells JOHNNY ANCASTER

he's in love,

and this one's different

(and not just because Johnny Ancaster never hears Billy Ancaster use words like the words he just used)

and this one's complicated

(and not just because this one is married)

(--to be fair, they're all married)

no, this one's different

because the look in Billy Ancaster's little lady-killing eyes

says so without the saying so

his little lady-killing lips move

to subsequently say so.

So,

Johnny Ancaster

tells Billy Ancaster

he's a fucking idiot

(and not just because he fucking is)

he tells him

because he's hoping his words aren't wasted

on still-ringing ears,

head-trauma or energy-induced

lovings aside.

Words of wisdom are always absorbed,

if not appreciated

for offering fair warnings.

...

Johnny Ancaster
has a bit of a cough, tonight

and while that's not unusual
 considering
the copious amounts of weed
he's typically consuming,

the cough tonight isn't typical
--and this isn't the book for subtle
foreshadowing,
so turn the page
and enjoy a not-so-subtle reminder
the world we're in
is still fucked
and far harder
than even your most earnest
Ancaster
ever could.

JOHNNY FUCKING ANCASTER
IS VIOLENTLY ILL
AND HE SWEARS IT'S NOT COVID
WHEN IT CLEARLY FUCKING IS.

AND HE'S BEING
A LITTLE STUBBORN AND STUPID,
IF AND ONLY BECAUSE
STUBBORN AND STUPID
ARE TWO THINGS ANCASTERS DO
VERY VERY WELL.

BEING SICK,
NOT SO MUCH

AND SO IT'S DAYS WORTH OF
COLD SWEATS
AND HOT SOUPS,

REFLECTING ON THE CHOICES
THAT LED HIM HERE,
LYING IN A SHEET-SOAKED BED
AND WONDERING
IF MAYBE THERE'S SOMETHING TO
THIS IMAGINARY PANDEMIC-THING
AFTER ALL.

Johnny Ancaster
might be the first
person in the country
to have Flurona,

he's that sick
and sick of
this latest lockdown
he's found himself in
bed and maybe sleeping
through,
and when he's awake
he's calling with
profound meditations
as to why

both Billy and Johnny
Ancaster
tend to pandemic
alone,
no one to care for them
when unforeseen
variants
up and overcome them.

"We need to do things
a little different"

proclaims **Johnny Ancaster**

boldy and from

the not-so-sanct sanctity

of his COVID-maybe deathbed.

Having made the first of many

bold proclamations

after realizing that

maybe living forever

isn't in the cards

the way near-death escapes

--and previously not-really-caring

if near-death escapes

were near or not at all--

have left him

both lying and thinking.

So he is,

Johnny Ancaster

both lying and thinking

and about the way they view the world

and all of the beautiful women

within it;

like maybe there's more

than selfishly motivated conquest

to courting

the fairer of the sexes

and for more than just sex

--like maybe there's something to

having someone there

to care

in ways that brothers just can't

when the proverbial chips are down

and this made up sickness

is making people

really fucking sick.

Johnny Ancaster
is on the mend
and from the Flurona
that more than likely
tried to kill him,

his furious anger
and the metabolic function that follows
more than likely
his sole saving grace.

Regardless,
Johnny Ancaster is back
and realizing
his lust for life
and the women that run/ruin his
deserve at least equally-angered
attentions

to the attentions he so attentively paid
them, collectively, before

the 'Rona tried to kill him.

So he's back,
Johnny Ancaster
and on the blunts
and no longer blunting
the more taciturn
of the tone he uses
when he picks up the phone to call them,

making up for both
lost time and
the lack of drama said lost time
must have mercifully allowed them.

Johnny Ancaster
has been in touch with a number of them,

women

and from his past,

and one, in particular,
takes an interest in
his recovery

reconnecting
over
shared calamities,

because as it turns out
she's recovering, too.

So the first Friday
he's on his feet and able

he's hosting
Lizzy-Come-Lately,

a former lover
and

one who always had
that particular kind of patience

needed for guys like him.

So

JOHNNY ANCASTER

tells BILLY ANCASTER

he's in love,

and this one's different

(and not just because Billy Ancaster never hears Johnny Ancaster use words like the words he just used)

and this one's complicated

(and not just because this one is back, and off the blocked-for-the-better-part-of-the-last-year list)

no, this one's different

because the look in Johnny Ancaster's little pitbull-looking eyes

says so without the saying so

his puffy little pitbull lips move

to subsequently say so.

So,

Billy Ancaster

tells Johnny Ancaster

he's a fucking idiot

(and not just because he fucking is)

he tells him

because he's hoping his words aren't wasted, and not just because this is turning out to be somewhat of a previously uncharacteristic pattern with the Ancaster brothers but because brothers are nothing

if not overly concerned for one another.

So Johnny takes the advice,

but not quite as good as he gives it,

absorbing more than just weed smoke when Billy tells Johnny he loves him

because he's man enough to admit it

and he hopes it works out for him

because he really hopes it does.

...

It turns out
Lizzy-Come-Lately
is good for
Johnny Fucking Ancaster.

I mean, they fight
but fighting with Johnny Fucking
Ancaster
is just what people do.

Between impassioned battlings
and bi-weekly breakups
that always seemingly result in
bi-weekly make-ups

they spend almost every waking minute
attached to the weekends she drives down
in

doing the kinds of things
people connecting post-Covid
tend to do,

so lots of being places
and doing things
and enjoying the company
old flings and new perspectives

tend to provide.

Which is fine by brash Billy

because he's left
with more time to take out recent
hurtings
on Other Married Women

doing the kinds of things
that really shouldn't have him wondering

how he ends up the alone
this book has already
spent pages in
the foretelling.

PART FIVE

The Other Married Women

Billy Ancaster fucks them

like he hates them.

And the irony is

he doesn't hate them at all.

Quite the opposite

though the hatred isn't internal either

(--because, as Billy Ancaster will attest, no one will or could ever love Billy Ancaster as much as Billy Ancaster loves Billy Ancaster) he fucks them

like he hates where he comes from

and he fucks them

like he hates where he's going

and like he hates where this night
is going

five seconds after

said fucking is done.

"What's this one about?"

...

Blowjobs

&

Boxing.

HIM IN THE RING HER IN THE BED

HE TAKES IT OUT ON EACH EQUALLY

EXPRESSING EXTERNALLY
WARS ORIGINATING OPPOSITE

AND OPPOSING ALMOST EVERYTHING
THAT MAKES THE MISTAKE

OF CROSSING HIM

RIGHT CROSSES,

OR WRONG GAZES.

Married women do it better

and their husbands won't tell you so

because their husbands aren't the ones getting fucked.

*actually, wait.

They are getting fucked.

Just in non-sexual, 'do-it-better, what's-that?'

ways.

He goes for those

otherwise committed

maybe because

committed

is about the only word he

does not believe in

The other married women matter

just maybe not enough
for their very own section
in this very book.

This very book
would be way too big,
honestly if not modestly,

if he had secrets for, say

HER

the one who took his heart
and his hometown
way before
it was fashionable
for the pain needed to fashion
books like this one.

There are books about her,
and
to be honest,
part of every book hereafter
will have a little part of her in it,

but by this book,
she's the kind of married
that means

while she loves him
very very much

she's more than likely

never coming back

*winky face emoji

because she might,
but not by the time
this book comes out

and so this book
is about the messes he's made
since she took up and
took his hometown.

...

Who could forget about

Her

married—and to Jesus (!)

which told bold Billy Ancaster
she was a sinner

well before she fucked around
and really proved it.

HE REMEMBERS
HER

FIRST OF THE MARRIED WOMEN
WHO WENT OFF AND HAD A KID OR TWO

AND THEN REMEMBERED
SHE LOVED BOLD BILLY

COMING BACK AFTER
ALL THESE YEARS

AND FUCKING AROUND
WITH
MORE THAN THE STABILITY
OF HER STABLE LITTLE HOUSEHOLD

FUCKING WITH
BOLD BILLY AND
FORGETTING WHY
SHE WAS SMART TO TRY AND STAY AWAY
ALL THOSE YEARS AGO

She

had a husband he knows
and knows quite well,

and he liked him, even

--he just liked her
a little bit more.

Her.

he had fun with
and her husband
was a nice enough
guy
he just
preferred
the closed-door
encounters
he found himself
encountering
on nights
attached to
the days
she should have
been at home with
him.

She
wanted to move from Arizona
so he called her AZ
anything but easy
with those big blue eyes
and the kind of
wild energy
that made her looking for homes
in towns adjacent to his
the kind of good idea
it probably really wasn't.

She was distractingly beautiful
and he loved her job and her voice and
might have maybe loved her, too

but his wild
mixed a little wrong with her wild

and so his international experiment
ended in the kind of tiny tragedy
all of the stories about women in these pages
tend to.

Her

he called co-worker
and he never called her
but still she came over
and left her husband at
home

reinforcing with every
other headboard-rattling
thought of reinforcing his
headboard that
his previously ascertained
assertion that marriage,
like love,
is simply not to be either
had or trusted.

Thoughts of

Her

he would like to keep all to

himself

DM me
for a semi-serious
seriously-dangerous
&
only initially

good time.

PART SIX

Fighting

Ten Round Tyson.

Ten-round Tyson
looks a little like Billy,
and I'm talking before the
matching black eyes
and bloody noses.

He could be
the Third Ancaster Brother
and he fights like it too,

beating brave Billy
like big brothers
almost always
beat brothers, smaller.

So it's not like there is
no love there,
beatings administered
on both ends
with a begrudging mutual respect
usually reserved for

those who share blood
on more than
shared white towels.

...

BILLY ANCASTER
GETS HIS NOSE BROKEN
ROUND TWO
OF A TEN-ROUND FIGHT.

AND DESPITE COMMON SENSE
AND A DATE ON SUNDAY

HE TAKES TWENTY FOUR
MORE
MINUTES OF PUNCHES
TO HEAVILY-BLEEDING PARTS OF FACES

FACING DOWN DEMONS

AND WHATEVER THE HELL ELSE

THESE VS TYSON FRIDAY-NIGHT
FIGHTS

HAVE STIRRED UP
IN BILLY ANCASTER

AND WELL BEFORE
BROKEN NOSES
AND SAID
BLEEDINGS.

...

IT WAS A LEFT HOOK
THAT PUNCHED A HOLE IN
BRAVE BILLY ANCASTER'S
PRETTY LITTLE HEAD.

A LEFT HOOK
OR LEFT HOOK, RIGHT CROSS
DAMNED IF BILLY CAN REMEMBER

THE WAY LEFT HOOKS HAVE LEFT BRAVE BILLY

STRUGGLING TO REMEMBER VERY MUCH AT ALL.

SO IT'S LESS ABOUT PUNCHES

AND MORE ABOUT REPERCUSSIONS

BECAUSE ALTHOUGH IT WOULD BE CONVENIENT

CONCUSSIONS AND THE SUBSEQUENT RASH DECISIONS

CONCUSSIONS TEND TO CAUSE

CAN'T BE FULLY BLAMED

FOR THE BAD DECISIONS UNFOLDING ON EVERY PAGE

THAT FOLLOWS THIS ONE.

BEHOLD
BRAVE BILLY ANCASTER

ALL CROOKED NOSE
AND
CROOKED SMILE
AND
CHOCK-FUCKING FULL
OF
THE KINDS OF CROOKED DEEDS
SAID SMILE LET HIM GET AWAY
WITH
SOME PUNCHES BEFORE FORTY
AND THE KIND OF CROOKED
LEFT LEANING NOSES
AND RAPIDLY LEAVING WOMEN
SEEM TO HAVE LEFT HIM TO

REMINDING BRAVE BILLY
ANCASTER
IN MIRRORS BOTH REAL AND
IMAGINED
THAT NO ONE GETS AWAY
CLEAN,

LEAST OF ALL
POOR
BRAVE BILLY ANCASTER.

Head trauma
is only in the movies

brave Billy Ancaster tells himself

in between the bleeding
he's currently bleeding
post-boxing
and on white towels
that quite frankly can't take it.

And maybe it amuses him,
the thought of white towels
throwing in the proverbial towel

signaling the end of fights
they can no longer take,

white towels
increasingly pink

when they emerge from super-necessary washes

on next mornings he feels
increasingly dizzy awakening in.

...

Want to quit
with every blank page
so you're welcome
for two-hundred-something
tiny testaments
to my stubbornness.

Want to quit

every time he steps through the ropes

but ten rounds
and
twenty bruises after

he's reasonably sure he made the right decision.

maybe the mirror
fights back harder
than Ten-Round Tyson

(although the wounds still-and-barely
healing from Friday last scream loudly
in their collective begging to differ)

regardless,
Billy Ancaster

finds one
decidedly harder

to still-swollen
face these days.

...

HE FIGHTS
MORE THAN HE WRITES
THESE DAYS

AND MAYBE BECAUSE
THE LATTER
HITS HARDER
THAN THE FORMER

SURFACE LEVEL BRUISING
HEALS FASTER

AND THE BROKEN NOSE
AND THE CRACKED RIBS
AND THE HOLE IN HIS FUCKING SKULL

CUMULATIVELY
ARE OF LESSER CONCERN
THAN FACING DOWN

THE REASONS
THEY LEAVE HIM

AND TO THE
WRITING

HE LEAVES FOR THE NIGHTS
ATTACHED TO THE DAYS

HE CAN COME EVEN CLOSE
TO FACING THE RESAONS WHY.

PART SEVEN

lockdown 4

BECAUSE BEHAVING IN A PANDEMIC
IS SOMETHING NO RESTLESS SOUL
SHOULD EVEN REMOTELY ATTEMPT TO DO.

The pharmacy is giving out booster shots
of various essential vaccines
and so Billy Ancaster takes
the jab
between scouring the coffee aisle
for coffee pods
and forgetting the first of
the essentials he'll inevitably
return for.

The booster shot
made everyone he knows
feel the kind of horrible
this prolonged pandemic
pretty much has them used to

but 10 round Billy
is in the ring
the very next night
trading punches
and theories
as to why
the punches, physical
hurt less and leave fewer marks
than the hits he's taken from
her
that drove him to tonight and
this ring
and
said feelings
to begin with.

Covid cases
go up in winter

because that's what
fucking Covid cases
do,

and while Billy Ancaster
is nothing if not brave,

he can't help but wonder
if he can take the hit on the chin

(proverbial or otherwise)

another rash of
rashly-decided upon government
lockdowns

will have upon a
psyche

black and blue
and marred from more than just

the repeated head trauma
and the repeated leavings
that maybe caused it.

So winter is dark
and more than metaphorically

and Billy waits
alone on the couch he once shared

for tidings that portent doom
this New Year less fun that the last.

THE GOVERNMENT
ANNOUNCED LOCKDOWN
NUMBER FOUR
TODAY,
AND IT'S FOUR TOO MANY
AND IT'S FAR TOO OFTEN
AND THE LAST THREE YEARS
HAVE LEFT THE BROTHERS
ANCASTER
DESPONDENT AND MAYBE
A LITTLE DEPRAVED,
AND
--AS EXCUSES GO--
IT'S NOT THE BEST

BUT IN LIEU OF THE REST
OF THE ADMITTEDLY
ATROCIOUS BEHAVIOR
IN THE PAGES BOTH BEFORE
AND AFTER THIS ONE,

IT WILL JUST HAVE TO DO.

...

THE LOCKDOWN
HAS LEFT HIM ALONE
TONIGHT

ALONE IN A LOCKDOWN
WHILE THE WOMEN HE
ENTERTAINS
AND ENTERTAIN HIM
ARE CUDDLED UP ON
COUCHES
LESS EXPENSIVE BUT
BETTER EQUIPPED
WITH PEOPLE TO
CUDDLE.

AND SO EACH AND
EVERY
ALL OF THEM
ARE UP ON THE
PROVERBIAL SEESAW

HE CLIMBED ON
MAYBE KNOWING
HE WOULD LOSE

CHILDHOOD GAMES
RESULTING IN
NOTHING MORE THAN
LONELY NIGHTS
ATOP UNCUDDLED AND
DECIDEDLY COLDER
COUCHES.

Billy Ancaster

tragically/inevitably

spends his holidays alone

self-imposed & externally obligated

isolations

do little for still-healing hearts,

while working wonders for

still-mending noses.

So Christmas hits harder

than the left hooks that left him here

lying in bed alone

and

maybe to himself when he

closes

still-swollen eyes and

pretends

it's anything remotely close

to okay.

...

THE PLACE I'M FROM
ISN'T A PLACE
AND
THE CITY I CLAIM
IS SO SICK
AND OF ALL OF THIS
AND NOT FROM THE PANDEMIC
BUT FROM THE HYSTERIA AND FAKE SHIT
THIS PANDEMIC REALLY WROUGHT
LESS SICKNESS
MORE PROPAGANDA

LIKE WHEN DO WE
COLLECTIVELY CLAIM
KEEP YOUR SUBSIDIES
WE'RE HEAVY ON SOME
SEMBLANCE OF NORMAL SHIT

Billy Amaster

isn't so good
and woefully
equipped
to take the L's
passing days
are beginning to
impart.

PART EIGHT

Gypsy.

That gypsy
has a boyfriend

but
Billy Ancaster
doesn't care
and maybe that gypsy
likes Billy Ancaster
just enough to not care, too.

And so she's over, that gypsy
and on expensive couches and
in between sips of semi-expensive
gin

she makes the mistake
they all make
in surprisingly similar
circumstances,

assuming brave Billy Ancaster
is anything other than as-
advertised

on surfaces cleaner than
the well-worn leather
she rests

her well-appointed ass upon.

...

The gypsy
is beautiful
really,

and despite being
really really beautiful
she's not
the self-absorbed
the self-absorbed women
he tends to fall for
typically tend to be

she's sensitive
like him, and
although bold Billy Ancaster
would never admit such a thing
he's the most sensitive boy
in the whole wide world

and so
the gypsy
is his kind of girl, for reasons beyond
her very real beauty.

The gypsy
is otherwise committed,
which is really kind of his thing too,

so beyond
her big brown eyes
and her big brown boyfriend
bold Billy Ancaster
likes her for reasons
beyond the reasonable reasons
he typically tends to.

She spends time, mercifully
and unmercifully it's never enough
to satisfy the utterly unsatiable
needs of bold Billy,

forever alone and
always on the nights
she doesn't grace him
with her graceful presence.

He tells her he understands,
other commitments and all,
but the utterly unreasonable
little lion in him
roars every night
she's anywhere but
beside/atop him.

WE'RE IN TRAFFIC AND
YOU'RE NOT ON MY LAP
ONLY BECAUSE OF THE SIZE OF THE
CENTER CONSOLE
AND THE CORRESPONDING SIZE OF
YOUR BIG FAT ASS,

AND I'M NOTHING IF NOT
HERE FOR
THE PLACES YOUR HAND IS PROBING

WONDERING LESS
ABOUT HOW WE'LL GET OUT OF
THIS MOTHERFUCKING TRAFFIC JAM

AND
WONDERING MORE
ABOUT HOW WE'LL GET OUT OF
THE CIRCUMSTANCES SURROUNDING
THIS LITTLE TRIP WE'VE SNUCK OFF
TO HAVE TOGETHER

YOUR BOYFRIEND BACK HOME
EAGER TO MARRY YOU

AND
MAKE YOU THE 'UNAVAILABLE'
THE REST OF THE MARRIED WOMEN
I'M USED TO WASTING MY TIME ON

LEFT ME TO,
SO DON'T
LEAVE ME TOO

FOR NOW
STUCK WITH YOU

AND

FOR ONCE
GRATEFUL

FOR MOTHERFUCKING TRAFFIC.

...

SHE DRINKS GIN
WITH A PURPOSE

AND THAT PURPOSE
MIGHT JUST BE

FORGETTING THE REASONS
REAL AND ATTACHED TO DECIDEDLY LESS
COOL NAMES

THAT ALMOST PREVENTED
HER SHARING THIS COUCH

AND THIS GIN
WITH LITTLE OLD BILLY A.

He's been
drinking
her gypsy tears
since before
drinking
gypsy tears
was a thing.

*Actually, maybe it's better to say
he's been drinking her gypsy tears
long after
drinking gypsy tears was a thing

because drinking gypsy tears
seems like something
wild boys like him
did way back when.

**Either way, he drinks them,
and
in a laundry list of
really kinky things
he'd like to do with and to her,

drinking her tears
is by far the tamest.

SHE DRINKS GIN
LIKE MAYBE SOME SMALL PART OF HER
HATES THE WORLD
EVEN HALF AS MUCH
AS SHE QUIETLY UNDERSTANDS HE REALLY
DOES

STARING INTO HIS
STUPID BLACKENED EYES
AND MAYBE LOVING THE DANGER
IF NOT THE BOY

BECAUSE BILLY ANCASTER
COMES AS ADVERTISED
SCREAMING AT HER
WITH QUIET DESPERATION

SITTING THERE
AND NOT SCREAMING
ON THE COUCH HE WAITS FOR HER ATOP.

Her ass
is the kind
that's really just not,

hurting him
the way it does

looking at it
under the constricting fabric of those
jeans and
wondering

what it will take
bold Billy Ancaster
to uncover it

the way she
by the looks of her, lying ass up on the
other side of his frankly-ridiculously
expensive couch

really really wants him to

too.

SHE DRINKS GIN
FAST
BECAUSE SHE KNOWS SHE HAS TO GO

BEING HERE
WITH HIM
NOT THE PLACE SHE SUPPOSES SHE IS
SUPPOSED TO BE

SOMEBODY DECIDEDLY NOT HIM
WAITING BACK HOME

AND FOR HER TO COME

THE WAY BILLY ANCASTER
IS HOPING SHE COMES TOO

DIFFERENT SPELLING
DIFFERENT INTENTIONS

THE DECIDEDLY DARKER OF WHICH
HAVE AN INCREASINGLY OFTEN HABIT

OF KEEPING HER
HERE.

Her ass
doesn't make sense

and her eyes aren't so bad
either

big and brown
and looking at him

the way they have been, off and on
and for the better part of eight years

the wonderings behind them
likely related to

thoughts of why
supposedly brave Billy Ancaster

is taking so fucking long
to come out and tell her

the things about her
aside from her no-sense ass

he has come to appreciate.

The gypsy comes over
for the hat she pretends she
left here,
brave Billy's apartment
on a Tuesday afternoon
they both really should be
somewhere decidedly else.

They wrestle,
verbally
with the things they often
non-verbally
wrestle with,

frustration and energy and
contemplated and increasingly
surfacing vulnerabilities

surfacing
between sips of the Gin she's
come to expect
on the somehow always sunny
Tuesday afternoons
she spends her should-be-
somewhere-elses

with today-bashful Billy.

Twisting arms
metaphorically
for my one hour a week

twisting arms
literally
trying to get you to stay
past pre-determined and already
allocated times

and

he calls more than he should
on moments you're away
and from him
and the seemingly oppressive
amount of time he so seemingly requires

time you begrudgingly acknowledge
is better spent with
me
twisting arms and otherwise
intertwined
atop couches
and
only because
you remain a little too good-girl
for more than subtly-suggested
bed alternatives.

Monday night
mid-pandemic
and he waits for her
to come over
or
maybe at least call

--it's not like they had concrete plans,
what with her having a particularly
needy boyfriend, and all

but tentative plans are the closest he
gets anways,
and she is
nothing if not (*surprisingly) tentative
even after all these years
of him being the (*only) other guy,

and so his Monday ends
the kind of disappointing
Monday nights
mid-pandemic
unsurprisingly and yet still
disappointingly

almost always end.

...

She says he's taking her down South
somewhere
and
the somewhere is where he comes from
and
the why is some really poorly kept secret
about how we plans to marry her

or
at the very least, begin the process
with the presentation of some ring, or
something

--listening to her,
there on the couch they cuddle on,
bold Billy can't be bothered
with wonderings and as to the ceremonies
attached
to silly circumstances he doesn't
understand

and
he believes her,
the way he always believes her

but some small part of him wonders

--of all the fights he's always fighting
this is probably the one
and for her
and for his place in her life

he really probably should.

He lets her leave,

couches and countries, bound for
somewhere South and so obviously better,

because when it comes for fighting for
the things he deserves
that aren't attached to brain-damaging
beatings

brave Billy

really isn't that brave,

after all.

...

You're The Only One I Can Talk To

on some

You're The Only One I Can Talk to

shit,

and the ____ty thing of it is,

we can't talk anymore

your need to

go off and get married

to some guy who isn't me

leaves The Only Therapy I Know

to empty couches and really good DVSN songs.

*Do It Well, DVSN. Go listen to that shit.

You're gin
she's whiskey
(big fan of both)
one burns a little more
one presents a little sweet
both
slowly kill the same.

the gypsy is gone
and he misses her,

and he takes her leaving

like the last left from Ten-Round Tyson

he can possibly take,

last crack

in an already

completely cracked skull.

...

PART NINE

non denominational Yearnings

Balenciaga bags are cool and all

--but have you tried not pissing them off in the first place?

(*apologies are increasingly expensive.)

WE BOTH KNOW I LIED WHEN I SAID I DIDN'T LIKE THAT TAYLOR SWIFT SONG.

We're here because we believed the things we told ourselves about each other.

...

I'M NOT WHO YOU COME HOME TO
WHEN YOU WANT HAPPY OR FULFILLED
OR FOREVER

OR ANY OF THE OTHER THINGS
A MAN WITH THE QUALITIES I
CLEARLY LACK
CAN GIVE YOU

NO,

I'M WHO YOU COME TO
WHEN YOU'RE SAD
AND YOU'RE LONELY

AND YOU'RE FEELING ALL OF THE
FEELINGS
WE BOTH KNOW I'VE GOT PLENTY OF

PLENTY OF,

AND MORE THAN HAPPY TO SHARE.

I DON'T CARE WHERE

JUST FAR

CHINO USED TO SING
BACK WHEN ANGST WAS JUST SOMETHING
PEOPLE OLDER THAN

YOUNG BILLY ANCASTER

SANG ABOUT ON
THE SAD SONGS
HE SOMEHOW ALWAYS KNEW
WOULD END UP BEING
ALL ABOUT HIM.

Is there anything better
in this whole wide world
coffee after whiskey
after
aching after you.

She's dry humping him
on his really expensive couch,
but all Billy Ancaster can think about
is the leaving
that's the last thing
on her horny little mind.

And so this one
is more about where his goes,
mind on matters other than
the admittedly important matter
mattering atop him right now.

It's insight, maybe
that mid-grind reminder that
the reader in you might maybe appreciate,
like maybe there's more to
our brave Billy Ancasater
than receiving admittedly-attention-
worthy grindings

from the enthusiastic if otherwise
committed
women,

women like the woman
enthusiastically demanding the totality
of his attentions
from her position atop astonishingly,
(*really!) expensive couches.

Tell me something
sweet,
it's been a bad
year
-or two
-or three
and
this badly
breaking heart
can't take
the more direct
of your break-my
-heart

breaking my
heart
words.

Needed You then

not so much now

someday in the not so distant

future

his tombstone reads

HERE LIES brave BILLY ANCASTER

he never got over it

Call me
DaddyWordsSoGood.

Quasi Over It.

The Weeknd came early
like Abel dropped on Thursday
and bold Billy Ancaster awaits
the inevitable arrival of the DMs
that will determine the direction
not even Thursday debauchery
will most certainly take him

...

*Equal parts out to getcha
and terrified you'll really get me.*

IT'S LATE
BECAUSE THAT'S WHEN THE WRITING COMES
AND
EASIER AFTER THAT SECOND GLASS
OF SOMETHING STRONG
AND ENOUGH
TO MAKE THE MIND SETTLE
ON
SOMETHING WORTH SETTLING ON

SCRATCHING AT BOTH
OLD WOUNDS
AND THE MOON
AND WONDERING
WHY I PICKED UP THE PEN
TO BOTHER WITH ANY
OF THE WONDERINGS
A STILL WANDERING MIND
AND TOO MUCH WHISKEY
MAKE A TROUBLED MIND
WANDER TO
RESTLESSLY
ON THE WAY
TO THE INEVITABLE
AND ALL-CONSUMING
EVENTUAL AND LONG-LINGERING
THOUGHTS ABOUT YOU.

...

~~He~~ wonders,

~~Billy does~~

what happens

when sad lions

get long

in well - gnashed

and once - mighty

teeth

IF YOU'RE READING THIS
YOU KNOW THE REST
BECAUSE CHANCES ARE
WE HAVEN'T TALKED
SINCE YOU MADE
WHAT YOU'RE HOLDING IN YOUR HANDS
THE KIND OF REAL
MY HAND AND THE HOLDING OF
NEVER REALLY COULD BE.

Ruined this too.

latest and last

of the pretty porcelain

finery

unfortunately left

in his China-shop path.

The revelation of
well-repressed
vulnerabilities
left him
the alone he
feared
every single
time.

Fuck You, money

steady waiting on

Fuck You money.

WAIT ...
LEARNING FROM MISTAKES IS A THING
PEOPLE ACTUALLY DO?

Stay

no subtext.

We both know I lied
when I said I can take it.

Baby,
you can't take enough belfies on your
last-year's-model phone

to begin to make it up to me.

Real good at writing
not so much at corresponding

so take this
as a too-late-to-matter
apology

and for the worst of
the lesser well-intentioned words
wasted in the throwing
at you in hopes of

holding onto that little bit of hope
you used to have about me.

...

Reservations are for

restaurants

so fuck it

come over

PART TEN

Inevitable & Ill-Timed Endings

Big Red stays out West
and she never visits
and while she DMs, from time to time,
the time between DMs is getting longer,
like the days,

Spring slowly coming and no immediate end
to this pandemic or this hell
in sight

and he's losing
sight and in his mind's eye

of the little things,
like what she looked like
and in particular
the look on her pretty little face
back when she used to tell him
she loved him.

She doesn't
love him, or at least tell him,
so much anymore

and maybe the head trauma
does him a favor
in the slow and steady
forgetting
of her face
and
the little details
surrounding the big words

Big Red used to lovingly
say to him.

Doomed doesn't message so much
these days

filled with the longing and regret
that follow
the kind of burning that particular
situation down
the way bad Billy did.

She didn't stay married,
the way they both knew she wouldn't

talks of working on her marriage
believable only in the sense
he got
that she really wanted to
and
that she really tried.

She didn't really
try
and with Billy Ancaster,

and his ill-timed words didn't help,

but Spring is supposedly coming
and Billy Ancaster is grateful for the
warmth of the sun

he'll need to replace
the warmth he used to find
between the lines

in the messages she used to
bother to message him.

Johnny Fucking Ancaster settles down
with Lizzy-Come-Lately,
a surprise to both
Ancasters and
the appropriately named
Lizzy herself.

He's displaying
a remarkable sense of
maturity,
post Flurona

maybe wizening the way
obnoxious Ancasters
seemingly never could

and so his Spring
looks decidedly better than his fall,
full of long walks and
the blunts he can smoke
out on them.

And while Billy is happy for him
he's maybe a little envious, too

and of the companionship
Johnny enjoys and Billy blows up

each and every chance he can,

setting fire to settling

like Johnny sets fire to his next and
appropriately timed

pre-rolled marijuana cigarette.

The Other Married Women stay
married
and
happily *

and
only come around
Brave Billy Ancaster
when it suits their fancy.

So
often
and enough to confuse him
as to both their intentions
and their continued desire
to stay married,

when
staying married
so often leads them
into his rotation
and
on occasion and for some,
into his bed.

Still,
Billy doesn't ask
because Billy doesn't bother

his heart
the broken and decidedly-elsewhere
some pre-married woman took it

way back when she took his hometown.

(*no such thing.)

Ten-Round Tyson is actually
the most stable motherfucker
in this whole book,

married and happily
and father to a litter of
future world title contenders
just like him.

He still boxes,
and Brave Billy,

but head holes and associated trauma
have settled their frequency,

if not their violence

on occasions where
boxing occurs.

So Spring is coming
and looking better
for Ten-Round Tyson,

should the pandemic part
and allow him the free reign
needed to resume

boxing everyone other than
not-doing-so-hot

Brave Billy.

Lockdown 4 kind of ends,
kind of doesn't

this "new normal"
anything but
and
never ending

and
although it has little to do
with the various leavings

burnt out Billy Ancaster
can't help but wonder
if anything can outlast

the sadness he assumes
almost everyone
except the ones who leave him

must most certainly
be left feeling

anxiously awaiting
whatever comes

after lockdown 4
and before

the seemingly inevitable arrival
of fucking lockdown 5.

~~Gypsy~~ goes off and gets engaged,
Bolivia
or
Venezuela
or
somewhere equally warmer than
here,
the winter Billy Ancaster
waits for word
that she's officially
leaving him, too.

She's happy
and
so he's

--fuck that,
he's not happy about any of it,
or for any of them,

his Spring
coming decidedly darker
than the collective outcome

coming out of the lockdown
described on the previous page

coming for everyone
even remotely associated with him.

So the gypsy goes
the way they all go

--away--

and Billy Ancaster can't even begin to
understand

why and why
he should bother to pretend
to be okay with any of it.

Non Denominational Yearnings aren't helping

Billy Ancaster deal
with the void
collective leavings
have left him to deal with.

He returns to the things he knows best,

writing

and about the various maladies
currently manifesting themselves
in the corner of his brain
that haven't been
boxed in

and

boxing

and to cope with the various maladies
currently manifesting themselves in the
corner of his brain

Ten-Round Tyson
hasn't beaten to death.

And he's close to death,
Brave Billy,

and he doesn't really realize it,
because that hole in his head

he really should have followed up on,

instead of following up on
the various loves

who couldn't wait to leave him.

Billy Arooster might make Spring,
but not long after

broken hearts and skulls
taking the toll

broken hearts and skulls
seemingly always tend to,

when tending to neither
result in days following the morning he
maybe doesn't wake up,

fresh off the last
nights

like last night,
the night he tossed and turned

about missing the pretty girls

he misses,

one of which,

*if you're reading this

is most likely

you.

(*it's too late)

THE END
...of brave Billy Ancaster
?

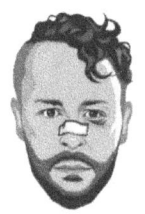

THE END

AND ONLY UNTIL

ANOTHER ONE
MAKES ME WRITE

ANOTHER ONE.

www.ingramcontent.com/pod-product-compliance
Lightning Source LLC
Chambersburg PA
CBHW072140100526
44589CB00015B/2011